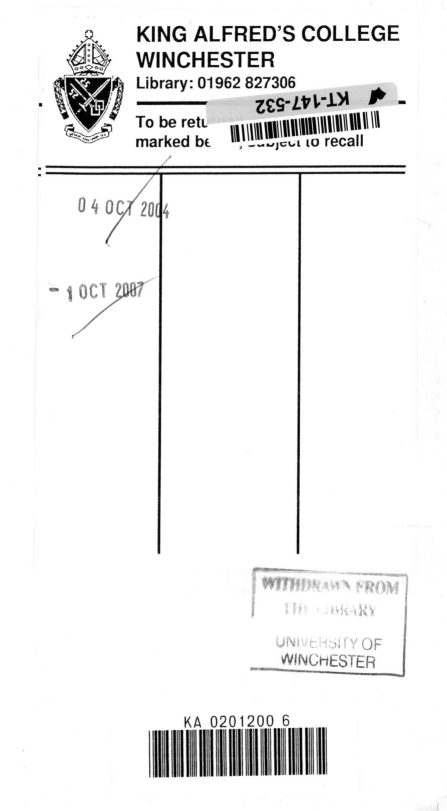

THE TRIAL OF LUTHER

by
DANIEL OLIVIER

translated by
JOHN TONKIN

MOWBRAYS
LONDON & OXFORD

© *Librairie Arthème Fayard* 1971

English translation first published 1978
by A. R. Mowbray & Co Ltd
Saint Thomas House,
Becket Street, Oxford OX1 1SJ

ISBN 0 264 66230 X

Typeset by Cotswold Typesetting Ltd, Gloucester
and Printed in Great Britain by
Redwood Burn Ltd, Trowbridge

Contents

Foreword by Professor Gordon Rupp   *page* vii

Translator's Preface   ix

Author's Preface   xi

1   Crusade Fever   1

2   Martin Luther   5

3   Albert of Brandenburg   12

4   Scandal   16

5   Letter to the Pope   24

6   Luther Indicted   29

7   Warrant for Arrest   33

8   Frederick the Wise   38

9   Cajetan   45

10   Farewell to Wittenberg   61

11   Commissioner Miltitz   76

12   Stalemate   85

13   The Leipzig Dispute   93

14   The Universities' Verdict   104

15   Germany to Luther's Aid   112

16   Leo X   117

17   The New Mahomet's Koran   127

18   Nuncio Aleander's Cross   137

19   The Battlefield of Worms   152

20   Charles the Fifth   160

21   The Death-throes of Unity   170

22   The Outlaw   179

23   The Stranger at the 'Black Bear'   187

Foreword

I am delighted to know that Daniel Olivier's brilliant and perceptive study of the trial of Luther should be about to appear in English. It is a masterly example of how a short essay with timely illustrations can compress great argument and I regard this as a most valuable piece of work. That it should come from a Catholic scholar is another good sign of our ecumenical times. Dr Tonkin who has translated this work is well qualified to do so, both from the distinction of his own writings on the Protestant Reformation and from his special study of Catholic attitudes to Luther in the last century. I hope this work will be very widely read. It deserves to be.

Gordon Rupp F.B.A., D.D.
Dixie Professor of Ecclesiastical History
University of Cambridge

Translator's Preface

This book was first drawn to my attention by Professor Gordon Rupp while I was studying under his supervision in Cambridge on a fellowship from the Nuffield Foundation.

At the time, I was engaged on a study of the very rich tradition of Roman Catholic Luther-interpretation, of which this book was an outstanding recent example. Like many recent Catholic works on Luther, however, its merit clearly lay not in any specifically Catholic perspective which it brought to bear on the subject-matter, but simply in its intrinsic qualities of historical and theological insight.

Father Olivier's aim in this book is essentially a modest one. He makes no claim to the discovery of any new evidence on Luther's trial, but seeks only to offer a fresh perspective on the material so painstakingly assembled and solidly established by Luther-research over the past half-century. That he has succeeded magnificently in this task is, I venture to suggest, amply demonstrated throughout this little book. Like Rupp's little study, *Luther's Progress to the Diet of Worms*, Olivier's work shows that a vivid imagination can breathe new life into even the most familiar material, and that simplicity and profundity are not necessarily opposed. To the general reader, he offers a gripping narrative reminiscent of a good detective story, yet the serious student or specialist who looks for something more than this will continually be struck by the scholarly insight which is no less profound because it is so unobtrusive in its expression.

Father Olivier's style is highly distinctive and idiomatic and poses in an acute way the translator's perennial problem of reconciling the competing claims of fidelity to the letter and the spirit of the original. The spirit has always seemed to me to be ultimately more important, and there are many places where I have found it necessary to depart significantly from the author's wording in an attempt to retain the fundamental meaning and distinctive flavour of the original.

Though the final responsibility for the translation remains mine, I wish to record my thanks to a number of people who have greatly assisted me in this task – to Professor Rupp, who first drew the book to my attention and graciously consented to write a foreword to the English edition, to Mr Robert Campbell, a senior student in the Department of French Studies at the University of Western Australia, who gave a great deal of valuable linguistic advice, to my wife, Barbara, who read the translation with a critical eye and provided many invaluable suggestions, and above all, to the author himself, Father Olivier, who willingly and painstakingly clarified all points of difficulty encountered in the text, and whose lively interest in the English translation was in itself most encouraging and gratifying.

John Tonkin
History Department
University of Western Australia

Author's Preface

'Luther's Trial' is a legal dossier comprising hundreds of documents and thousands of pages. The condemned man made repeated appeals, and it would take a lawyer to decide whether he could have obtained a reversal of judgement.

This trial lasted four years, from 1517 to 1521. On the judges' bench, the presidency was held, successively, by Cardinal Cajetan, the theologian John Eck, Pope Leo X and the Emperor Charles V. The accused man, Martin Luther, underwent an extraordinary progression: in 1518, he showed himself to be more Catholic than the Pope; in 1519, he no longer believed the Pope to be a Catholic; in 1520, he became the prophet of a Christianity without a Pope. Yet a young twenty-year-old Catholic, Charles V, compelled him in 1521 to leave his spiritual homeland.

This modest essay attempts to capture, in a few swift strokes, the confrontation of these two intransigent positions. It is not possible to include everything, but we hope we have given at least a sufficiently objective version of this morality-play. By acknowledging the manifest good faith of the players we understand the compelling cause which each one was arguing. The collision, in the last analysis, was between two irreconcilable conceptions of Christianity – irreconcilable, in that no way could be found, in this battle for the redemption of the human conscience, for the pontiff and prophet to compromise.

Because the prophet's role is to reveal what is 'not yet seen' he bears scant respect, in this role, for Tradition. He is especially stubborn where he is presumed to know what he is talking about.

The pontiff, standing for order and the institution, fears

nothing more than disorder; he can see in the creative process nothing but chaos. As the appointed defender of doctrine, his role is to transmit faithfully the inheritance received from the past, and those who step beyond these limits are to him nothing but 'innovators'.

Surely a healthy Church is one in which the prophet can brush aside accepted conventions, in which his novelty enriches the tradition and grants it a new lease of life.

I

Crusade Fever

June 1517. The city of Rome was in a state of siege. The soldiers of the Church were holding the crossroads and patrolling the streets, ready to quell all seditious movements.

His Holiness Pope Leo X was holding counsel with his cardinals. Some of them were absent from the roll-call: their Eminences Riario, Dean of the Sacred College, Petrucci and Sauli, lay in the dungeons of the Castel Sant'Angelo, accused of conspiracy, waiting for the Holy Father's verdict.

Leo X was determined to deprive those who elected the Pope of any desire or opportunity of getting rid of him. Torture had extracted from the accused the disturbing fact that other cardinals were implicated in the conspiracy.

Leo X was the son of Lorenzo the Magnificent, the distinguished ruler of Florence. Destined from birth for a career in the Church, he had been made a cardinal at the age of thirteen by Pope Innocent VIII (who, in return, had acquired for his own son the hand of Maddalena, the sister of the young prince of the Church). At the conclave of 1513, after the death of Julius II, who had bequeathed to his successor a schism and a council, Giovanni de Medici had been the candidate of the youthful and, at first, of those who were now conspiring against him. Behind him lay a career of twenty-five years in the Roman Curia, which he knew like the back of his hand, and he felt sure he could unmask the other conspirators.

Each member of the consistory was invited to make a public confession, and the Pope knew exactly what to be content with; Cardinals Soderini and Castellesi were soon driven into a corner to confess their guilt and beg for pardon.

I

The secrecy which surrounded the deliberations of the supreme Senate of the Church did not prevent the city and the world from keeping abreast of its affairs. The accused men had many friends and allies so the matter had to be ended as quickly as possible. Some days later the Pope and the loyal cardinals held another session. It was a stormy one, lasting for some hours, and their deliberations were audible outside. Since the time of the Avignon Papacy, the College of Cardinals had grown in importance in the Church, and the sovereign pontiff could not dispose of its members at will, even when they were guilty. Leo X, nevertheless, was able to ensure that the traitors were stripped of their purple, deprived of their functions and heavily fined. All except for Petrucci, the moving spirit in the conspiracy. He had thought of using a dagger but then decided on poison: he knew that the Pope was suffering from a fistula in the anus, and hoped to accomplish his purpose with a carefully prepared ointment.

Petrucci had lost and would pay for it. On 27 June, some accomplices, for whom no one had wanted to invoke papal clemency, were executed, while the Cardinal himself – a mere twenty-seven years old – was soon afterwards secretly strangled.

This was not the first time that Leo X had had trouble with his cardinals. On his accession, he had had to bring back into line some of those who, with the French king's support, had re-convened the Council of Pisa with the aim of deposing Julius II. The two leaders, Carvajal and Sanseverino, had extricated themselves by publicly recanting their error. Giovanni de Medici's clemency had amazed the whole world, and overawed the fathers of the Lateran Council, the legitimate council which was destined to continue for another four years.

The unsuccessful attempt was a much more serious matter than Carvajal's schism, for it showed that the sovereign pontiff was not safe even among those who assisted him most closely in his task. They were not all assassins, far from it, even though death by dagger or poison was a daily event in Rome. But it was clear that in the heart of the sacred college there was a powerful party opposed to the Medicis that a monarch could conceivably entice again into a dangerous adventure.

By temperament, Giovanni de Medici was loath to act severely. He had too much political acumen not to understand that the humbling of the college of cardinals weakened the papacy itself. The solution did not lie there. The remedy for the chronic anti-papalism of the sacred college was to pack it out so that it would be impossible to organise an effective opposition. By swelling the cardinals' ranks with enough Medici partisans, the Pope would be assured of overwhelming support in all circumstances.

On the first of July, Leo X created at a stroke thirty-one new cardinals, more than the sacred college numbered at the time, and more than it had ever numbered. Among those elected were Thomas de Vio, General of the Dominicans, Adrian of Utrecht, the former tutor of the Spanish king, and some wealthy individuals, one of whom had given 30,000 ducats in exchange for the purple.

Having consolidated his position at the head of the Church, Leo X was now able to devote himself to the problem which had been paralysing his affairs of state for two years. In good Medici style, he had wanted to install his nephew Lorenzo as Duke of Urbino. But the legitimate duke would not allow himself to be dispossessed, and he conducted a war which was ruining the Holy See's treasury. Once again the Pope had to squander the gold for which he was begging throughout Europe.

In the autumn the problem of the crusade against Sultan Suleiman came up. This was to be the great project of his reign, and the council which had ended in March had called for action. Since the capture of Constantinople in 1453, the Turks had been spreading across Europe, the Mediterranean and the Balkans; and wherever Islam established itself, the Church withdrew. The Pope's duty was to defend Christendom by mobilizing the Christian nations against their common enemy. In fact, it was a matter of persuading the German Emperor Maximilian, and the kings of France, England, Spain and Portugal to conclude a treaty among themselves and to confront together the Turkish peril. Only the Pope could be supreme head of this campaign, and Leo expected much of it: it would make him the arbiter of European politics.

On 19 October, Cardinal de Medici, a cousin of the Pope and what today we would call 'Secretary of State', asked for the help of the Venetian navy. On 4 November, a commission of cardinals was formed to finalise a plan of attack. Less than two weeks later a detailed memorandum was sent to the chancelleries concerned. The estimate came to 800,000 ducats, which was double the annual revenue of the Papal States. The Pope in any case did not dream for a moment of financing the cost of the enterprise himself. A tithe would be established throughout Christendom, and preachers would explain to the faithful the importance of the sacrifice which was being asked of them.

But Christian people had for some years been contributing towards the heavy expenses of the construction of the Basilica of St Peter in Rome. The money was levied by means of a kind of 'street collection'; preachers offered indulgences, letters of absolution, butter-letters (permission to eat butter during Lent) and other favours and privileges, in exchange for which everyone gave an offering according to his means. There were murmurs that the Pope and his court thought only of enriching themselves on the backs of the faithful.

Leo X, in fact, was extravagant and ostentatious, like the great Renaissance prince he was. The Church's coffers were continually being emptied by war and by the arts, not to mention 'petty pleasures'. That was the weak point of his pontificate, the Achilles-heel of his power.

Some days before Christmas, the German courier brought a message from the Archbishop of Mainz: a monk named Martin Luther had just raised the standard against indulgences.

An entirely different crusade was beginning.

2
Martin Luther

'Our Lord Jesus Christ willed that the whole life of the Christian should be a life of repentance. . . . The penalty of sin remains as long as man is truly penitent. . . . The Pope neither can nor wants to remit penalties other than those which he himself has imposed. . . . The transformation of ecclesiastical penalties into penalties of purgatory is a tare which must have been sown while bishops slept. . . . Men are deceived when they are told that as soon as the coin clinks in the coffer, the soul leaps from purgatory into heaven. . . .'

The nervous and incisive little phrases flowed one after the other from the scratching pen. They were not really assertions; rather queries, question marks. Doctor Luther was trying to make a diagnosis. His speciality was holy Scripture, the Bible. By dint of reading it and meditating upon it, he had just identified the evil with which, in the opinion of many, the Church was wounding itself. Christian life had become a series of formulas: good works, pilgrimages, indulgences. The Bible showed, on the contrary, that there was one 'work' alone: faith.

Indulgences lulled the conscience to sleep. They were an insurance for the hereafter. Introduced in the era of the first crusades for certain limited cases, they had been unreasonably extended and had falsified the people's scale of values. Men wanted at all costs to escape the punishment of sin after death, namely, purgatory and hell. This was made possible by an offering, in exchange for which a man would receive a piece of paper granting absolution from hell, or a voucher for so many days or years less purgatory. Those who paid were thereby set free.

To be sure, the Church required a spiritual disposition on the part of the penitent. But the official doctrine was that the Pope had the power to draw at will on the infinite treasures of the merits of Christ, the Virgin and the saints in order thereby to benefit the faithful. Martin Luther doubted whether the indulgences were truly useful. They turned man away from what was essential, the imitation of the suffering Christ, the love of the poor, the rejection of self-interest.

'Every true Christian has a share in the treasures of Christ and the Church. . . . This sharing is given him by God even without letters of indulgence. . . . It is difficult to preach indulgences and true contrition at the same time. . . . Christians must be taught that it does not conform with the Pope's thinking to place on the same footing the sale of indulgences and good works. . . . They must be taught that he who gives to the poor and lends to him who has need does better than he who buys an indulgence. . . . The Pope's indulgences are useful if one does not rely on them. But they are disastrous when they result in the loss of the fear of God. . . . If the Pope knew the abuses of the indulgence preachers, he would prefer to see St Peter's basilica reduced to ashes than to see it built with the skin, flesh and bones of his flock. . . . They are enemies of Christ and the Pope who silence the Word of God in the churches to make way for the preaching of indulgences. . . . The true treasure of the Church is the Gospel of the glory and the grace of God.'

The solitary writer saw a vision. Banners shimmering in the sunlight, all the candles alight, a procession moving towards the indulgence preacher, voices singing the ancient canticles. Children were there with their teachers on holiday. Men had deserted their workshops, women had interrupted their housework to swell the ranks of the parade. They were followed by the city council, the burgomaster at the head, monks and priests. The precious scrolls, the object of so much greed, were at the city gate, guarded by another group of priests, treasurers and secretaries, not to mention men at arms. The bells rang out a full peal – then came the triumphant entry into the church, the thunder of the organ. A scarlet cross was raised in the middle of the nave, adorned with streamers in papal colours. . .

'To say that the cross solemnly draped in papal colours is as efficacious as Christ's own cross is a blasphemy.'

This was indeed what was being told to the worthy people. At Jüterbog, some distance away from the Augustinian monastery in Wittenberg, where Luther was trying to sort out his nagging problem, a Dominican friar, renowned for his extravagance, was brandishing letters of indulgence like an itinerant pedlar. Father Tetzel had missed his vocation.

The faithful came again and again to the monastery to ask for explanations, some begging for the absolution for which they had gained the right through a handful of small change. Others were disturbed by this mysterious grace bought by the living for the profit of the dead – why hadn't the Pope had the charity to empty purgatory in one stroke if he had the power to do it for money? Was it necessary to go on paying for masses for the dead when a plenary indulgence for the deceased had been obtained? Was the Church going to repay the money for these masses performed to no purpose? If the Pope allowed an impious man to pay for the eternal rest of a pious man, could he not himself spontaneously grant the same grace to this soul? Was it honest to assist the sale of a new indulgence by suspending the effectiveness of those already granted?

So many questions were added to the list that in the end it comprised nearly a hundred points for discussion: ninety-five to be exact. These 'theses' would normally have served as the basis for a university disputation. A month earlier Doctor Luther had started off an exchange of views on the theology taught in the universities of Christendom in a similar way.

But deep down he sensed that he would not be satisfied with a purely academic gesture. Since the day in October 1512 when, at the age of twenty-nine, he had put on a doctor of theology's cap, he considered he had a twofold duty: to the truth which the Church required him to defend and to the people, redeemed by the blood of Christ. The preaching of indulgences was injurious to the truth and to the people. The officially acknowledged purpose was that the Pope needed money for the construction of St Peter's in Rome. But what did this Medici do with his money, this heir of one of the greatest fortunes of Italy? Did the ambitions of an empire-building pope justify the distribution of divine grace at a discount?

Doctor Luther possessed the text of the instructions given to the preachers by the Archbishop of Magdeburg, in whose name the indulgence auction was taking place. It seemed that the instructions were to obtain above all a quick return. In fact, the Archbishop seemed to be unconcerned about Tetzel's methods and devices. It was enough that the Dominican was effective.

A scandal could have broken out any day, not everyone could be fooled. Meanwhile a scandal already existed in the degradation of the Christian ideal under the patronage of the highest spiritual authorities.

For a long time, Luther felt he should intervene directly with the Archbishop of Magdeburg. Wittenberg was within the jurisdiction of his archbishopric, and there was nothing unusual in a monk entrusted with the teaching of theology confronting the hierarchy with a problem which was at once doctrinal and pastoral. But the prelate was a man of substance. The brother of the Margrave of Brandenburg, he had recently been designated Archbishop of Mainz, so making him head of the German Church, and he also bore the political titles of Electoral Prince and High-chancellor of the Empire. Doctor Luther had no experience of the world of politics or the life of the court. In putting himself forward, he was entering an unknown world.

Unable to measure in advance the consequences of his action which would inevitably have political repercussions, he had not spoken up until now. Because of this indecision, he felt himself becoming more and more at odds with himself. If a doctor of theology shrank from a doctrinal problem which seemed to him both serious and urgent, he should resign. But one did not resign a mission.

On 31 October 1517, the eve of the festival of all the saints whose merits were up for auction, Luther at last set down on paper the phrases burning in his heart and on his lips.

'Wittenberg, on the eve of All Saints, 1517'

'To His Excellency Lord Albert, Marquess of Brandenburg, Archbishop of Magdeburg, Archbishop-Primate of Mainz.

'Reverend Father in Christ, illustrious Prince,

'May your Highness forgive me, the least of all men, for having the temerity to write to you. The Lord Jesus is my witness that I have long hesitated, conscious of my weakness and unworthiness, in doing what I now dare to do today. What constrains me to do this is the loyal obligation that I owe to your Highness. May you cast a favourable glance on one who is but dust and look favourably on my request.

'Under your distinguished name, papal indulgences are offered all over the land, for the construction of St Peter's. I do not wish to complain so much about the shouting of the indulgence preachers, which I haven't heard. But I deplore the false idea it gives to the people, and which these preachers propagate everywhere. These unhappy souls believe that if they buy letters of indulgence, they are assured of salvation; they believe also that souls escape from purgatory as soon as a coin is dropped into the chest. The grace obtained through these indulgences will be such that every sin, however great, can be absolved, even if someone (to use their own words) had raped the mother of God. Finally, they believe that man is delivered by indulgences from all penalty and guilt.

'It is in this way that the souls committed to your care, excellent Father, learn to journey towards their death. And thus your heavy responsibility constantly increases towards those for whom you have to render an account. This is why I can no longer be silent. For no man can receive assurance of his salvation through some bishop, when he is not even assured of receiving it by God's grace. The Apostle enjoins us to work out our salvation constantly in fear and trembling, and only the just through affliction will be saved. The road to eternal life is narrow. Everywhere the Lord proclaims the difficulty of salvation.

'Works of piety and love are infinitely better than indulgences, and yet they are not preached with such display and effort. They are passed over in silence so that indulgences can be preached. A bishop's chief duty is to see that the people hear the Gospel and the love of Christ. What a disgrace, what a danger for a bishop if, with the Gospel passed over in silence, he permits the uproar of indulgences to resound among his people and is more preoccupied with that than with the Gospel. Will not Christ say to those who have done this: "You strain out a gnat, but swallow a camel."

'I will go even further. In the instructions for the indulgence commissioners published under your name it is said (surely without your knowledge and approval) that one of the principal graces is that inestimable gift of God, by virtue of which man is reconciled with God, and by which all the penalties of purgatory are wiped out. It is also said that contrition is not necessary for those who acquire indulgences and letters of confession.

'What can I do, revered leader and illustrious Prince, but beg your Highness, in the name of the Lord Jesus Christ, to deign to give this matter your fatherly attention, to cancel these instructions and to impose on the indulgence preachers another method of preaching? Unless this is done, someone may rise up to refute in public both these preachers and this little book, thus bringing disgrace on your Highness. I would be deeply disturbed at this, but I fear greatly that it will happen if no prompt remedy is forthcoming.

'I pray that your Highness will accept this good office of his humble servant, with all the kindness which becomes a bishop and a prince. For I also am a sheep of your flock. The Lord Jesus guard and protect your Highness now and in eternity. Amen!

'Your Highness will be able to examine my theses here attached, and see how questionable is this doctrine of indulgences.

'Your unworthy servant, Martin Luther, Augustinian monk, doctor in theology.'

Doctor Luther was content. He had succeeded in expressing exactly the apprehension which had finally made him speak up. The scandal of indulgences could go on no longer. Perhaps Albert of Brandenburg would intervene, or some other person would do what was necessary on his behalf. Luther knew that this 'other' would be himself.

The time had come to lift religious practice out of its rut. Everything seemed to indicate that the hour had struck. The ecumenical council had ended in March without remedying the evil, and the Holy Spirit would have to seek another instrument from within the people of God. Nothing could prevent the coming of what must come. This was what the Archbishop must understand, but Luther hardly dared to believe that he would.

He felt himself to be absolutely alone in this course dictated by his conscience, and he wanted it this way. No one should know anything, not even his friend Spalatin, the priest who exercised the functions of chaplain and secretary to the Elector of Saxony in the court at Wittenberg. Only the bishop, Schulze, his immediate superior, would have a copy of his letter to Magdeburg. This was a precaution against anyone attributing to Luther what he had not said and did not wish to say.

3
Albert of Brandenburg

In the absence of the Archbishop, who was detained in his Rhineland diocese, it was his assistants who dealt with Doctor Luther's message. At first sight, it seemed nothing very serious. Just another monk's attack on indulgences!

However, disquieting rumours were circulating. The theses of this fellow Luther seemed to have been made public and the people were restless. It was said that the Elector of Saxony was not unaware of the affair. Of the professors of the University of Wittenberg, the electoral capital, Doctor Luther was one of those most in the public eye.

At the council of 17 November this was the only problem under discussion. Agitation had increased, and this was imperilling the current financial operation. For the indulgence preachers, at Jüterbog and in the region, were working on behalf of the Archbishop of Magdeburg and Mainz, who was at the time administrator of the diocese of Halberstadt. He had only been able to accumulate these three dignities by turning over to the Holy See some 30,000 ducats. He would surely recoup this sum in due course, for his three dioceses were rich. But Rome would not wait, and he had found it necessary to advance the money, money which he did not have. On an earlier occasion, the bank of the Fugger brothers of Augsburg had paid off his taxes to the Roman Curia. But the Fuggers charged 20 per cent interest, so the debt had to be liquidated as quickly as possible. The Curia had been understanding enough to suggest that the Archbishop superintend the indulgence preaching in the regions under his jurisdiction. Everyone would gain from that; given the impetus by a prelate on the spot, the campaign for the construction of St Peter's in Rome would yield still more, and the Pope would leave half the profit to the new prince-bishop of Mainz. The latter would not even need to lower himself to work unworthy of his station: the Fuggers would be responsible for having the preachers followed and deducting their due as the work proceeded. It was only necessary for Albert of Brandenburg to name a high commissioner for indulgences, such as the Dominican John Tetzel, an energetic man who had much experience of this kind of work, and who knew how to talk to the people.

The Wittenberg professor's protest threatened to upset the whole scheme from the moment it found a favourable echo in popular opinion. The Archbishop risked being under the control of the powerful Augsburg bankers for a long time. It was scarcely credible that the monk had acted on his own authority. The University of Wittenberg had been founded by the Elector of Saxony, whose aim in creating it was to enhance the prestige of his capital and his principality. A university attracted scholars and students, and made it possible to exercise influence in the Church. The Elector had already forbidden the preaching of the indulgence in his territory, and now seemed to want to throw 'his' University into the struggle he had long been waging against the house of Brandenburg. No doubt about it, the problem was a political one.

This reasoning relied on the striking contrast between the decline of the Saxon dynasty and the irresistible rise of the Hohenzollern family, which was installed not only at Brandenburg, but also in Pomerania, Schleswig-Holstein, East Prussia, and now at Mainz; while since the end of the preceding century Saxony had been divided between Duke George, who ruled at Dresden and Leipzig, and his cousin the Elector Frederick the Wise, whose 'capital' was only a miserable little village of two thousand souls.

But Duke Frederick was an electoral prince of the Holy Roman Empire, and because of this he had good reason for thwarting the capture of Mainz by Brandenburg. The constitution of Germany, that is to say, of the 'Holy Roman Empire of the German Nation', in fact provided that the Emperor should be elected by seven electors, four lay princes, the King of Bohemia, the Duke of Saxony, the Margrave of Brandenburg (whose capital was Berlin) and the Count Palatine; and three ecclesiastical princes, the Archbishops of Mainz, Cologne and Trier. Albert of Brandenburg was the younger brother of the Margrave Joachim. On succeeding to the see of Mainz, he became the second elector in the family, which meant two out of seven. Now Frederick was being considered as a candidate for the imperial crown, when the Emperor Maximilian should die. . . .

For the canons of Magdeburg, there was only one thing to be done: they had to inform their master as quickly as possible of the new situation created by the Wittenberg people. So Doctor Luther's dispatch now took the road from Aschaffenbourg to the Rhineland, where the Archbishop was living.

Raised to the episcopate at the age of twenty-three, thanks to his family's power and the Emperor's protection, Albert of Brandenburg was no theologian. Since the right of primogeniture gave his brother the succession of Brandenburg, he had to seek his future in an ecclesiastical career. Fortune had smiled on him, for at twenty-four years of age he was, so to speak, three times bishop; and the diocese of Mainz, whose territory stretched as far as Halle and Erfurt in the heart of Germany, was by far the largest of the three ecclesiastical electorates.

Albert found the monk's letter impertinent. But, he told his counsellors, he was not concerned with the tedious outpourings of this professor. He did not even want to be worried by the machinations of the Elector of Saxony. However, as there was a risk that ignorant people would be shocked and led into error, it was necessary to do something, and the simplest step was to forbid any public statements on indulgences. Nothing was easier than for the primate of Germany to silence the troublemaker. And, since the man boasted of his status as a doctor of theology, the University of Mainz, which was older than that of Wittenberg, would examine his theses.

At the beginning of December, Albert of Mainz received the support of the masters of his theology faculty. They made special reference to Luther's pronounced opposition to papal power. The Wittenburg doctor limited the competence of the sovereign pontiff in the matter of dispensing indulgences; and that was contrary to the dogma of primacy.

For a man who had reached the peak of the German ecclesiastical hierarchy before the age of thirty, there was a great temptation to demonstrate his capabilities to Rome. Albert had put his finger on what seemed to be indeed a heresy; his vigilance had not been found wanting. Though he was not competent to intervene personally in doctrinal affairs, he fancied that he could impress the Holy See. He wrote to the Pope that the 'holy business' of the indulgences had been taken to task by a monk, whose writings (those which were in his possession) he was enclosing. The doctors of the University of Mainz detected in them a certain odour of heresy. But it did not seem necessary to consider a canonical condemnation. Perhaps an admonition. . . .

Then the Archbishop told the Curia of his diocese of Magdeburg that the affair had been passed on to Rome. The chancellery would be advised to make contact with the Reverend Father Tetzel so that he could prohibit any publication on the question, pending the reply of the Holy See. But they should avoid provoking a conflict with the Eremite order of St Augustine, to which Luther belonged.

4
Scandal

The distance between Magdeburg and Wittenberg was not so great that one would have to wait weeks for an acknowledgement of a letter. In the end Luther despaired of getting anywhere with the ecclesiastical authorities. In fact, he never received a reply. The episcopal Curia of Magdeburg took the view that Mainz did not want anyone to trouble any more with this affair and simply shelved it. Tetzel was not even warned.

However, Luther had taken another initiative which lay behind the reports made to Albert of Brandenburg by his counsellors: as part of his duties at the university, he had tried to start the debate which appeared to him to be more indispensable than ever. The doctrine of indulgences posed a great number of questions, and it was the theologian's business to reply to them. He had therefore posted his theses on the theology faculty's noticeboard and informed some of the experts in the neighbourhood. He intended to provoke a far-reaching discussion to determine the principles behind a practice of which the Church had never really given a coherent account. The theses were not, strictly speaking, 'conclusions'; following the common usage of all the universities, they aimed at eliciting an exchange of views. Their worth could be measured only by the richness of the debate which they would eventually make possible. Doubtless, some of them would not be discussed, while others would only draw attention to minor points which should not be forgotten. The doctor who took the initiative and responsibility for a disputation of this kind had the greatest latitude in formulating his propositions. He was not expected to be 'orthodox', but to know how to bring about the best possible discussion. Paradoxes were permissible and even highly valued. After the debate the originator of the dispute would draw out the apparent solution and formulate his conclusions.

To Luther's immense surprise nobody showed up. Instead, by a chain of entirely unforeseeable circumstances, the debate intended for the University took place in the public square. What happened was that the printers got hold of the text of the theses. They were in Latin, the language of theology, but soon they had been translated and disseminated throughout Germany. In a matter of weeks people were talking of nothing but the 'scandal' which had just broken out at Wittenberg. The affair got out of Luther's control.

The man most directly affected by this fracas was the preacher Tetzel who met increasing hostility as a result of Luther's theses, which the public took at face value without worrying about their original meaning. The Dominican reacted forcefully. Sure of himself, and armed also with the powers of inquisition, he was not going to be intimidated by a simple doctor: 'This heretic must be thrown to the flames within three weeks!'

At his request the University of Frankfurt-on-the-Oder, in Brandenburg, drew up a list of 106 theses refuting Luther's assertions. A debate took place in January under the presidency of the high commissioner, after which Luther was denounced to Rome for heresy, while from the pulpit preachers predicted his impending death at the stake.

A young nobleman in the service of the Archbishop of Mainz wrote to a friend:

'Have you heard the news? At Wittenberg, in Saxony, there is a revolt against the Pope's authority. It's the monks who are in the thick of the action, and other monks are trying to do them in. They are weeping, roaring, and crying out to heaven. Some of them are running around the libraries writing great learned tomes on the affair. They are selling theses and counter-theses, conclusions and vitriolic pamphlets. Let's hope that these brawlers will wipe each other out.'

Luther looked on, powerless against the racing tide. In March, his students burned several hundred copies of Tetzel's theses, snatched from a street vendor. He declared that he was in no way in favour of all this which was in fact the truth; but nobody believed him.

His correspondents from Nuremberg drew to his attention an opinion on his theses, given by his friend John Eck to the Bishop of Eichstatt. Eck, the Vice-Chancellor of the University of Ingolstadt, pointed to a number of assertions which, according to him, showed Luther's opposition to papal power. Luther was astounded, and hastily drafted a reply which he sent privately to Eck. But one of his colleagues at Wittenberg, Dr Karlstadt, decided that the good name of the University had been damaged and unleashed a violent polemic against the professor from Ingolstadt.

Passions became so heated that Luther's friends tried to dissuade him from leaving for Heidelberg on the business of the Augustinian order. To travel such a distance would be virtual suicide, for Luther would certainly be arrested and taken to Rome, if not assassinated.

He shrugged his shoulders. 'What can I do about it if they want to believe anything they like about me? I can't stop the people talking; and it's not my place to forbid them. Let them say, hear and believe what they want, where they want and when they want. I will do what God gives me to do, and with his grace, I fear nothing.' Since his task as district vicar responsible for the monasteries in electoral Saxony required him to go to Heidelberg, he would go, and on foot.

His intervention on the indulgences had changed nothing about his life. Throughout the winter, he had gone on with his course on the Epistle to the Hebrews, expounding the Bible as the Church had commissioned him to do. During Lent, he preached nearly every day and, since the people had caught wind of his objections to the doctrine of indulgences, he published a sermon in which he showed where, in his view, the true answer to the problem of sin was to be found.

The Elector had made known that he would take Luther and Karlstadt under his protection, that under no circumstances would they be indicted; let alone deported. The Prince did not know Luther personally, but had heard him preach and knew him to be neither ignorant nor blasphemous. Anyone who dared to raise a hand against him would have to deal with his ruler. Luther's enemies knew this, and the sense of their powerlessness served only to stir up their anger.

Before setting out for Heidelberg, Luther wrote to his superior Staupitz, the Vicar-General of the Observants in Germany, who had always held Luther in great esteem. When Luther had entered the order in 1505, fresh from the University of Erfurt, he had attracted notice by his docility and piety, and Staupitz had come to regard him as a man who would pass on his own spiritual ideal in the Church. As early as 1512, when Luther was 29, he had set him to work for the degree of doctor of theology and had had him appointed by the Elector to the Chair of Holy Scripture in the University of Wittenberg.

Staupitz knew better than anyone the spirit in which the indulgence theses had been drawn up. In his view, the hostility against Luther was groundless, and the matter would finally be put right. Luther wasn't the only one to criticise indulgences. Others went in for far more violent attacks on papal power. Compared to the humanist Erasmus who, for some years, had been attacking monkish ignorance and superstition with his bantering and his witticisms, Luther was one of the purest manifestations of the current of renewal which was developing within the Church.

'Since I am overloaded with work,' Luther wrote, 'I cannot write to you at length. I do not find it difficult to believe what you tell me about my evil reputation. I have been reproached for a long time for condemning the rosary, the breviary, the psalter, and all good works. But that was once said of St Paul: "Let us do evil so that good will ensue." I am doing nothing in reality but following the theology of Tauler and of your little book on the love of God. My teaching is that we must place our confidence solely in Jesus Christ, and not in prayers, merits or good works. For our salvation will come not from our own ardour, but from God's mercy.

'It is from such observations as these that certain people have extracted the venom which they propagate on every hand. In deciding to act, I thought neither of my own glory nor of the trials I would have to undergo. Nor can these motives make me change my views. God will judge.

'They dislike me because I prefer the Church Fathers and the Bible to the scholastics. Some of them forget why. But I read the scholastics freely and not blindly like so many others. This is what the Apostle teaches: "Examine everything and retain what is good." I don't reject everything, but I don't approve everything either. If Scotus, Biel and company have allowed themselves to deviate from St Thomas, and if the Thomists are allowed to contradict everyone and each other, why shouldn't I state my case by the same right? If God is in the deed, nothing will stop it, but if it is not he who inspires us, nothing will come of it. Pray for me and for the truth of God, wherever it may be.'

Luther's sojourn at Heidelberg, where he presided over a disputation on grace, allowed him to assess both the broad influence of his ideas, and the depth of resistance they aroused. The young gave him an enthusiastic welcome, while his former teachers from Erfurt were more reserved.

On his return, he tried to explain in a letter to the eminent Doctor Trutvetter, one of those to whom he owed most.

'Don't think that I could be offended by you or that I should want to confuse you with sarcastic and hurtful letters, as you seem to believe. I don't even do that for those who are denouncing me in the pulpit as a heretic, a madman, a seducer, or a man possessed by the Devil.

'I thought that my doctrine might displease you. But I am not the only one to speak of grace and works as I do. You know the ability of our doctors – Karlstadt, Amsdorf, Schurf, Dr Wolfgang, Feldkirchen. They all share my ideas, as does the whole University, with the exception of the licentiate Sebastian; The Prince and our Bishop are on our side. Other prelates and men of learning are saying that for the first time they feel that someone is speaking to them of Christ and the Gospel.

'Allow me to share their judgement until the question is resolved by the Church. Frankly, I believe that it is impossible to reform the Church without radically weeding out canon law, the decretals, scholastic theology, philosophy and logic as they are treated at the moment and instituting other studies; I pray daily to my Lord that the pure study of the Bible and the Fathers shall be restored to honour. You don't consider me a logician, and perhaps I am not; but I fear no man's logic in defending this position.

'With regard to the theses about indulgences, I have written to you that I was not pleased by the fact that they were spread abroad. . . . In fact such an event is unheard of, and I could not foresee what would be the effect of such badly stated theses; otherwise, I would have drawn them up more clearly, as I did in the case of the German sermon which shocks you more than the theses themselves.

'Doesn't it disturb you that Christ's unfortunate people are tormented and fooled by indulgences? Does the remission of a temporal and arbitrary gratification justify putting the people's faith in jeopardy? For there is scarcely a man who doesn't believe that he can acquire by indulgences something as great as the grace of God. It was good that we ourselves first brought that into the open, lest the people would discover for themselves the indulgence traffickers' fraud – supposedly pious but in fact profoundly impious – and pay us back our just deserts. As for me, I admit that I wish that there were no indulgences in the Church – these indulgences which the Italians would avoid like the plague if they didn't lead to profitable livings.

'If you can still tolerate the advice of him who was your most obedient and devoted disciple, I would say this; it was from you that I first learned to trust only the canonical books, and to read the others with a free judgement, as St Augustine, and above all Paul and John prescribe.

'Grant me with respect to the scholastics the freedom which you and all the others have enjoyed until now. I want to follow the Scriptures and the Fathers of the Church as they bring me better teaching, and I will only listen to the scholastics when they support their propositions on the affirmations of the Church. And I do not intend to be turned aside from this opinion either by your authority, which carries great weight for me, or less still by that of any other person. I am ready to endure and to accept all your criticisms. However severe they are, they will appear very gentle to me.'

On returning to Wittenburg, he had to face the truth: the situation had worsened. From Staupitz he learned that Rome had taken offence at his theses, and that he was in danger of excommunication. In a few months, the anger of those who were exploiting indulgences had made him suspect and now he was a marked man.

Yet it was not especially of himself that he was thinking on 16 May when he preached a sermon on excommunication. This penalty was the most severe that the Church could inflict. It meant, in the first place, exclusion from the community of the faithful. But in a Christian society, it had tragic civil consequences; the excommunicate was stripped of his rights and eventually condemned to be burnt alive. Recently in Switzerland, four Dominicans had perished in this way.

Since the time of the Great Schism, when three popes had reigned simultaneously and mutually excommunicated each other and all their partisans, excommunication took place for the slightest reason. A creditor, for example, could have his debtor excommunicated to oblige him to pay up. The success of the indulgence preachers rested largely on the fact that they also handed out letters of absolution, allowing men to be rid of minor excommunications. For a modest offering, one could escape the consequences of sanctions used indiscriminately by clerics too full of their own power. No one could scorn a piece of paper which might be needed at any time.

For a long time Luther had been scandalised by these practices. His study of the Bible had brought him to understand that consciences did not depend so directly on the will of the clergy. He argued that excommunication did not automatically break community with Christ, for that deep community, founded on faith and hope and love, was beyond the reach of purely juridical resolution: men could not destroy what God had created. The outbreaks against the excommunication agents, in which so many of them had perished, would mean nothing when all men came to understand that no real injury could be done by those who abused a power which they did not possess; and that the injustice they caused did not harm the soul. 'If you are wrongfully struck down by excommunication, do not let yourself be turned from the action for which you are unjustly condemned. And even if you must die without sacraments and be buried like a dog, happy are you. Justice and your loyalty will earn you eternal reward.'

This sermon made a profound impression on lawyers and theologians, and it did not escape Tetzel's notice. No one had ever yet dared to speak like this. Some theses of a particularly extreme nature were extracted hastily from it, and circulated as if they came from Luther. What would the heresy-hunters say if they knew that only the intervention of Bishop Schulze and some friends had prevented Luther from opening a debate on this explosive subject?

5
Letter to the Pope

Taken aback by the unexpected distribution of his theses on indulgences and the agitation which they had provoked, Luther soon understood that he must immediately offer the public an explanation. Their text was intended for professional theologians and could barely be understood by the layman. Theologians alone could perceive the intentionally provocative little phrases and the debate which the questions were trying to draw out. Since the projected discussion had not taken place, Luther himself stated precisely the problem which he posed in each thesis and the kind of solution he envisaged. He worked on these *Explanations* in the early months of 1518.

His ultimate aim remained the same: to stir up a discussion which would be sufficiently far-reaching to halt a dishonourable practice which caused countless misunderstandings.

He could not launch this new publication in an already more than overheated setting without the authorization of Schulze who, as Bishop of Brandenburg, was Suffragan Bishop of Magdeburg and pastor of Wittenberg. The Bishop was at first reticent, but finally gave the green light and even made known his approval of the proposed doctrine. Strengthened by this episcopal approval, Luther fancied that he would strike a great blow by addressing the Pope in person.

Staupitz perhaps was aware of this decision. It was clear that Leo X was besieged by men who thought only of discrediting Luther and it was getting dangerous to let them do as they wished. In giving the Pope first-hand information, perhaps there would be a chance of diminishing the influence of his adversaries on the sovereign pontiff.

Luther thought that Leo's only desire was to put an end to the abuses brought to his attention. He imagined the Pope to be sensitive to the idea of the great scandal which would erupt when the faithful realised the transience of what was being offered to them in exchange for good money. He had a rather naive view of the Pope and doubted neither his honesty nor his zeal. The fact that the bishop of Rome was vicar of Christ was good enough for him. And he shared with many the idea that after the sensualist Alexander VI and the bloodthirsty Julius II, Giovanni de Medici had brought the papacy back to its true vocation. Accordingly on 31 May, Trinity Sunday, he sent off to Staupitz the following text, destined for the Pope.

'I have learned, most holy Father, that my reputation has been seriously maligned before you and your counsellors, as if I had undertaken to diminish the authority and power of the keys which belong to the sovereign pontiff. I am accused of being a heretic, an imposter and a traitor which leaves me overwhelmed with astonishment and horror. My sole consolation is my innocent and peaceful conscience. What I hear is said of me is not new, for I am treated no better in my own country. May you condescend, therefore, most Holy Father, to listen to the account of this affair from the mouth of a man destitute of culture and eloquence.

'Recently in our region the preaching of apostolic Jubilee indulgences began, and the preachers dared to teach publicly the worst godlessness and heresy, thereby bringing shame and derision on the power of the Church, as if the decretals which condemn abuses did not apply to them. Furthermore, not content with spreading their poison around in words, they published tracts and distributed them among the people. In these tracts (leaving aside the extraordinary and insatiable greed which emanates, so to speak, from each syllable) they asserted the same godlessness and the same heresies and they bound confessors by oath to impress them on the people in the surest and quickest way possible. This is the truth, and there is no way they can escape it; the tracts are there and they cannot deny them. Everything was going remarkably well, they were exploiting the people with false hopes and, as the prophet says, "they were tearing the flesh from their bones" while they indulged and fattened themselves with delicacies.

'Their sole means of avoiding scandal was the fear they inspired in your name, the threat of the stake and the shame attached to the name of heretic. It is hard to believe how ready they are to make such threats, when they sense the least opposition to their idle talk. Is this avoiding scandal, or is it not rather stirring up schism and sedition by tyrannical action?

'Malicious talk was just as much in evidence around their booths where they carried on their traffic: priests' greed was criticised, there were stirrings against the power of the keys and the authority of the sovereign pontiff – of this the whole countryside was witness. It was then that I became incensed with zeal for Christ, as it seemed to me (or, if you prefer, by a youthful ardour). It was not my place to decide or to act in this matter, so I addressed personal notices to a certain number of prelates, some of whom listened to me, while others thought me stupid. No one dared to intervene in an area under your authority. Seeing no other possibility, I decided to combat these traffickers, as best I could, by raising doubts about their doctrines and provoking a debate. So it was that I published my theses, inviting only very learned men to discuss them with me. Not even my adversaries could doubt that I made this point very clearly at the head of my list of theses.

'This, then, is the fire which (if one listens to them) is devouring the whole world with its flames. Perhaps it is doing so just because they refuse me, a doctor of theology by the grace of your apostolic authority, the right to debate in a public place of learning, in accordance with the custom of all the universities, not only about indulgences but also about things incomparably more important like the power of God, the remission of sins and divine mercy. It does not bother me very much that they refuse me this right which has been granted to me by your Holiness; for it must be well known that, on their side, they mix improperly the dreamings of Aristotle and theology, and speak pure nonsense about the divine majesty.

'By a miracle which astounded me more than anyone, these theses were spread through almost the entire world. I had published them according to the custom of our university, and drawn them up in such a way that I cannot believe that they could be understood by all. These were only theses, not theological assertions or articles of faith and, in accordance with the custom, they were presented obscurely and enigmatically. If I could have foreseen what would happen, I would certainly have taken care that they had been easier to understand.

'What am I to do? I cannot recant, and I see the hostility inspired by this publication let loose against me. Against my will, I am exposed to the perilous and changing judgement of public opinion, I who am a man destitute of learning, spirit and culture, in an age when letters and learning have known such a flowering that Cicero himself would be relegated to obscurity.

'In order to pacify my adversaries and in response to many people's wishes, I am publishing these *Explanations* to elucidate my theses. As a precaution, I am putting them under the protection of your name, most Holy Father, so that all those who wish may understand that I have always respected and revered the authority of the Church and the power of the keys and at the same time learn of injustice and duplicity of those of my opponents who have so injuriously overwhelmed me. If I was as they represent me, if I had not treated this whole affair correctly, conforming with the rules of disputation, the illustrious Prince and imperial Elector, Frederick of Saxony, would never have allowed such a nuisance in his University, and I would not have been tolerated by the masters of the same University who are so strict and zealous. I am acting openly, so that those sanctimonious rogues will be unable to cast disgrace either on me or at the same time on a prince and a University.

'Prostrate at your feet, most Holy Father, I offer myself to you with all that I am and possess. Make me live or die, say yes or no, approve or blame according to your pleasure. I recognize in your voice the voice of Christ, who reigns in you and speaks through your mouth. If I have deserved death, I will not refuse to die. "The earth is the Lord's, and the fullness of it." May he be blessed for ever and ever, amen, and keep you unto him eternally, Amen.'

Luther reminded Staupitz himself that it was his superior's advice which put him on the path of the doctrine which he was now defending; that the spirit of penitence was not the result of our efforts, but the effect in us of God's grace, that the Christian's calling was to live by the grace which has been given, not to seek to buy it.

It remained only to await the results of this new initiative. Luther dreamed that the Pope would uphold him in his battle for the Gospel.

6
Luther Indicted

At the very moment when the letter arrived at its destination, Leo X had just ordered the opening of proceedings against the Wittenberg monk. The German primate's warning had been taken with all the gravity which such an eminent person could expect, and the insistence of the German Dominicans convinced the Curia that the affair was serious.

The first dignitary to concern himself with the dossier, from the end of 1517, had been Cardinal Cajetan or, to use his proper name, Thomas de Vio, Superior-General of the Dominicans. He was the best theologian in Rome and, in the early years of Leo X's reign, he had distinguished himself by a brilliant defence of papal power. Luther's texts appeared to him to confirm the judgement of the University of Mainz. Moreover, he had discovered in them surprising and strange new views on the doctrine of the sacraments.

Following Cajetan's report on them, Cardinal de Medici had sent a papal order to Father Della Volta, the Provisional-General of the Augustinians. He must without further ado put his subordinate back on the right path, and smother the spark before the fire should flare up. At the Curia, they remembered Jan Hus of Prague, who had also begun by preaching against indulgences, with the result that for a century Bohemia had been put to the fire and the sword. The appearance of a similar movement in a neighbouring region gave grounds for fearing a new outbreak of troubles.

In March, a point by point denunciation of Luther by Tetzel had arrived. In his capacity as inquisitor, Tetzel had the right to pursue every suspect doctrine. He accused Luther of heresy and it needed no more than that to open proceedings.

The general chapter of the Dominicans, assembled at Rome towards the end of May, returned to the charge. The Saxon provincial reported the unrest and indignation which the doctrines of the Augustinian monk were stirring up in Germany. To put Tetzel on a par with Luther, it was decided to confer on him the rank of doctor of theology. And, since the Augustinians seemed to have done nothing with Cardinal de Medici's injunction, another 'preacher', Father Perusco, procurator of the Roman tribunals, was invited to do what was necessary for Luther to be finally indicted.

Luther's letter to the Pope and, in particular, his clarification of his theses, only aggravated his position. Instead of the retraction expected from him, he stubbornly held to the same errors. Perusco had all the reasons he needed for charging Luther with the propagation of doctrines opposed to the teaching of the Church.

An episcopal magistrate, Jerome Ghinucci, took charge of the briefing. He charged another Dominican, Sylvester Mazzolini, known also by the name of Prierias, to put in evidence the legal points which justified the present undertaking against Luther. As 'master of the Holy Palace', Prierias had the final say in the censoring of books. Three days were enough for him to draw up the report expected of him, which was to be published under the title *Dialogue on the daring assertions of Martin Luther regarding papal power*. It was easy to see how the proceedings were shaping. Luther criticised a practice, indulgences, but his judges thought only of charging him with a revolt against papal power.

Prierias' argument rested on the notion that the essence of the Church was the pope. The universal Church was, in a sense, nothing but the Church of Rome, the head of all the Churches. The Roman Church manifested itself above all in the college of cardinals, the principal dignitaries of the diocese of Rome. And, since the body of cardinals was nothing without its head, it was necessary that the Pope be understood, in certain respects, as being identical with the Universal Church. He was as infallible as the Church, with the same kind of infallibility as the Church. In saying that the Pope was going too far in the matter of indulgences, Luther was denying infallibility at any rate on this point. His theses were rash, erroneous, false and even heretical.

Armed with these conclusions, Ghinucci then drew up a summons against Luther. He must present himself at his hearing sixty days hence (to date from the moment when he was notified of this summons) in order to reply concerning his errors and his contempt for papal power. If he should refuse, he would be severely punished.

As it took some weeks to travel from Wittenberg to Rome, the accused would have only the time to make preparations and get on the road. That would stop all this talk about him.

The document was rushed to the Legate whom the Pope had just sent to the Emperor in Germany, none other than Cardinal Cajetan. His mission was to persuade his Majesty to take part in the crusade against the Turks. But as the Pope's personal representative he had an authority above that of the nuncio, Carraciolo, and the Archbishop of Mainz. All matters passed through his hands.

The negotiations in question took place in Augsburg, where the Diet, the periodic assembly of the rulers of the Empire, was held. The Legate was solemnly welcomed there on 7 July by Emperor Maximilian, to whom he presented the symbols of holy war, the helmet and the sword.

Maximilian responded favourably to the papal appeal, but he showed himself little disposed to impose the necessary taxes for financing the crusade. Cajetan gave assurances that the sums in question would serve no other purpose, but the Diet was suspicious. To make up for this the Emperor decided to deal severely with Luther, and he addressed a letter to the Pope

along those lines. The Legate thus had no difficulty in trans-
mitting Ghinucci's citation, along with Prierias' *Dialogue*. The
Elector of Saxony did what was necessary, and on 7 August
Luther found himself officially notified that he must appear at
Rome within two months. This period of grace soon started to
run out.

7
Warrant for Arrest

At the beginning of July the Count of Mansfeld, the overlord of the little town of Eisleben where Luther had been born in 1483, had recommended to the Augustinians that they should not allow their brother Martin Luther to leave Wittenberg any more. He had learned that Luther's enemies were preparing an ambush and would not hesitate to strangle him or cut his throat on the spot. The journey to Rome would multiply their opportunities and, even supposing that the Saxon monk should arrive safe and sound in the capital of the dagger and poison, one could easily imagine what fate lay in store for him there.

Nevertheless, Luther observed the threats raining down on his head with the greatest calm. Such a persecution for an entirely commonplace action in his life as a professor of theology seemed to him a sign from heaven. In the Bible there were many situations of the same kind. Men could endure the truth only up to a point, beyond which they saw red. Was this not the Lord Jesus showing him that he, like St Paul, would have to suffer much for his Name?

He felt that he was ready to endure everything. He had no wife or children in whose interests he had to take care of himself. He had already disposed of his property, house and goods through his monastic vows. His reputation and fame were every day a little worse off. That left his body, which was not in the best condition. If he were to be killed, his life would be shortened, perhaps by an hour or two, but no one could rob him of his soul.

What preoccupied him most was the Pope's silence. He had deluded himself, believing that he could get the Pope on his side, but his opponents had been more powerful. Didn't the Pope have anything to say about the Gospel?

The Elector gave no directive. He had his own worries. The Diet was like a basketful of crabs, where each one had to be constantly on guard to protect his own interests. Besides, it wasn't the prince's business to compromise himself, and by temperament he would not do so. His protection could be depended on, but it could only be exercised if legal means were found to stop the case Rome had begun. A minor sovereign was not big enough to do battle with the Pope; he would very soon be reduced to begging for mercy from the imperial power, the natural ally of the holy see.

The Emperor! He was the one to be worked on, for only he had the power to hold the Roman judges in check. But the master of the Empire himself could not reject out of hand an accusation coming from so high up. As things stood, the only conceivable manoeuvre was to get Rome to agree to give up the case and transfer it to a German tribunal. The Council of Basle had decided that Rome should automatically send back cases to the judicial authorities of the countries where they originated. In the present case, this procedure would be facilitated by the fact that the Dominicans, Luther's avowed enemies, held in their hands all the threads of the case; and their impartiality could legitimately be put in doubt.

Luther did not think for a moment of going to Rome, which was a little inconsistent with his professed detachment. It was not just a question of his personal safety; he wanted a reply on the matter of indulgences. Prierias' pamphlet seemed to him so feeble that he could not bring himself to take it seriously. It was simply not worthy of a reply. To go to Rome would be giving his opponents an opportunity to bury the affair, and the indulgence traffic would resume and increase. His protest was not going to be stifled without his taking a stand on the basic issues, and therefore he must at least gain time.

The decision was soon taken; in a letter to the Elector of Saxony, Luther asked him to ensure that his case be heard in a neutral place and by impartial judges. As it was essential that the prince be able to produce this letter, the plan which the accused had formed was transmitted to Spalatin.

The Elector's secretary should intervene with the prince and with Pfeffinger, the counsellor representing Saxony before the Emperor, to support the request for a transfer of the hearing to Germany. Frederick and the Emperor had to obtain papal consent. Spalatin must assert the interests of the University of Wittenberg and stress the partiality of the Roman judges. The 'Dominican murderers', in particular Prierias, had set themselves up as both judges and accusers, and the fair-minded Frederick would be aware of the anomaly of such a situation. As soon as he had succeeded, Spalatin should without delay inform Staupitz, the Vicar-general, and Luther himself who, while he awaited all this, would produce a refutation of Prierias' *Dialogue*.

The days went by and there was no news. Luther was waiting constantly for Frederick's decision. He learned that the Pope had formally ordered the Legate to settle the affair with the Emperor or the Elector, naturally at their expense. The Pope, the Emperor, the Cardinal-legate, the electoral Prince of Saxony, were up against a single man who was counting the days till he would have to choose between departure for Rome and contempt of the law. Through all this, Luther felt amazingly calm. Everything he had came from God. He did not wish to attribute anything to himself. If God should take away his liberty, nobody could protect him. But if God were leading him, no one could destroy him.

On 21 August he declared to Spalatin, who still had not replied, that he did not see how he would escape the threatened sanctions without the Elector's intervention. He preferred, however, to suffer his lot rather than to see his prince compromised on his account. The Elector had never been involved either way in this matter, and it was not for him to suffer the consequences. Not knowing what else he could do, Luther left it up to his correspondent.

'I accept in advance whatever you wish. I will never be a heretic. I can be mistaken in discussion, but I refuse to say just anything at all. I must not be asked simply to align myself to the opinions of men.'

His friends had thought out a way of saving him from his predicament. He could not go to Rome without a passport or safe-conduct from his ruler. The first reply to make to the Roman summons was therefore to lodge a request for such a document. The Prince would only have to refuse for purely administrative reasons, and Luther would have a convenient excuse. Luther suggested the plan to Spalatin without hoping too much of it.

The course of events was to justify such action. For when Spalatin received the message, developments at Rome and Augsburg had completely changed the situation.

The Emperor's letter on the Luther affair had been sent on 5 August. Maximilian asked the Curia for the monk's immediate excommunication on the grounds that he expressed himself in a manner which was heretical and worthy of condemnation not only about indulgences, but equally on the power of excommunication. His ideas could dangerously infect the ignorant people as well as powerful princes. The Holy Father could be assured that everything would be done to carry out his sentence.

To the charges about the theses on indulgences were now added the fruits of the campaign of defamation Tetzel's party had been conducting since May, derived from the sermon on excommunication. Besides the fabricated 'theses' on excommunication, they produced a fierce and equally fraudulent epigram against Roman avarice. The whole thing had had a disastrous effect in Augsburg.

The Emperor's indignation and the existence of new evidence had encouraged the legate Cajetan to ask Rome for an intensification of the measures already taken. The judges did not hesitate; without waiting for the time given to Luther to expire, they declared him a notorious heretic, which allowed them to order his immediate arrest, and they had orders drawn up to send to the authorities concerned: the Legate, the Elector of Saxony, and the Saxon provincial of the Augustinians, of whom Staupitz was only the subordinate.

On 23 August the most important of these documents was ready. It was a 'brief' (paradoxically a very long one) to Cardinal Cajetan, giving him the authority to have the heretic arrested, and to place him in safe custody, while he awaited new instructions. The Elector, for his part, was invited to hand over the 'son of perdition'. For good measure, the Augustinians were ordered to send to Saxony one of their number armed with the power to seize the 'heretic and schismatic Martin Luther' and put him in chains. Father Della Volta improved on these instructions and let it be known on 25 August to Father Hecker, the Saxon provincial, that he was himself summoning Luther to Rome as a rebel against his authority.

In the summer of 1518, the noose swiftly tightened around the agitator's neck. He had only a few days of freedom left.

8
Frederick the Wise

The Elector Frederick had not remained indifferent to Luther's anxieties. A charge of heresy was not to be taken lightly, and as a statesman, the prince knew what a scourge heresy represented. Saxony was Bohemia's neighbour and the Hussite wars had not spared her. Frederick was a man of sincere and rather fearful piety and had no doubt that he would deal severely with Luther if the latter should be convicted of error against the faith.

But what was the accusation about? It began with Luther's intervention against the indulgences, a traffic organized by a Dominican under the protection of the Archbishop of Mainz. The reaction to Luther was clearly inspired by self-interest and anger. It took a doctrinal form at the University of Frankfurt-on-the-Oder, which was a rival of Wittenberg and under the Elector of Brandenburg's jurisdiction. This political and university rivalry was increased by the antagonism between Augustinian and Dominican teachers. Dominicans were in evidence at all stages of the proceedings. It was by similar proceedings that the Dominicans had been trying for years to do away with the learned scholar Reuchlin, proceedings which the Pope himself had finally adjourned. Thus it was not enough that the Dominicans accused someone of heresy for people to have to believe them.

Luther's doctrine appeared no more novel than that of the great Erasmus, who was in favour with Rome and who led the intellectuals of the humanist stream. Luther's criticisms were not unprecedented, and he himself was rather moderate. His writings were not even comparable to the virulent pamphlet

Letters of Obscure Men which had come out the year before. So it was not for his criticisms that he was being blamed.

The University of Wittenberg would certainly be annoyed if Luther were found guilty of heresy. Men in whom the Elector had every confidence, the Vicar-general Staupitz, his own secretary Spalatin, vouched for Luther's doctrine. Everything suggested that Frederick should not make a hasty decision.

The summons to Rome, however, required that some immediate steps be taken, and Luther's sovereign had to ensure that they were carried out. Frederick was not happy at the prospect of removing the most prominent man in his university; not was he resigned to handing such an easy victory to the Hohenzollern party. His sense of justice made it a duty to defend any subject of his who was suspected without cause. But it was difficult for him to find, on the spur of the moment, a way of warding off a blow from the formidable power of Rome. Besides, the Diet posed many problems. . . .

He decided to wait, as was his custom. There were sixty days before him. It was more than he needed to examine the thousand and one possibilities of delay which this law offered. It was not too difficult for one of the great men of the Empire to find a way of intervening without being found out.

The Emperor and the Diet daily confronted a host of political questions, of which the most important was that of succession to the imperial throne. Maximilian was getting on for sixty and he felt his end approaching. He wanted to pass on the crown to his young grandson Charles, the young Burgundian prince who at the age of sixteen had just ascended the throne of Spain and Naples. But the Empire was not hereditary. The succession depended on the electors. The house of Habsburg, however, had been able to keep the crown for some generations, and Maximilian was determined not to let it go. He himself had been elected when his father was still alive, and he wanted to repeat this precedent.

The main obstacle was the Pope. Rome did not want an

emperor who would hold the combined power of the Holy Roman Empire and of Spain. For the papal State would find itself in a pincer-situation between the Spanish possessions of southern Italy and the German feudal territories in the north of the peninsula.

The legate Cajetan was instructed to prevent the election of Charles of Spain at all costs. He put forward an excellent case; for centuries, papal policy had insisted on the principle that the King of Naples could not also be King of the Romans. But 'King of the Romans' was the principal title of the German Emperor ever since the papacy, as mistress of the West, had given the former Roman Empire to Charlemagne and his successors.

The role of the electors was solely to designate the one who would bear the crown. To carry the title of 'Emperor', the chosen man had to be crowned afterwards by the Pope, in Italy. The Holy See, was, therefore, able effectively to oppose the succession of an undesirable king; it could be impossible to bring Charles of Spain to the imperial throne if the Pope refused in advance to crown him. . . .

Accordingly, Maximilian tried to manipulate the Curia. His zeal for a crusade and for stamping out Luther's nascent heresy was not entirely disinterested. His declarations, moreover, pledged him to nothing. Without the money which the Diet refused to the Legate, the crusade project must be abortive. And, since the Emperor had to treat the electors with caution, he could not contemplate taking up arms against Frederick if the latter refused to hand Luther over.

Even though he might try to gain the assent of Rome if it cost no effort, he decided to disregard any opposition from the Curia. Maximilian could, on the other hand, do nothing without the electors and he would have to bring together at any rate most of them to support Charles' candidature. Now a majority was already secured for another candidate: Francis I, King of France, the most powerful vassal of the Holy Roman Empire since his victory at Marignano in 1515, which had made him master of Milan. The two Hohenzollerns, the Archbishop of Trier and the Count Palatine, were pledged to elect the King of France. Francis, who had at his command the troops of Franz Von Sickingen and the Duke of Wurttemberg, was in the position to secure his rights when the moment came.

French gold poured in like a flood, and Maximilian in turn had to dig into his own coffers. The electors were quite willing to be bought; it was necessary only to fix the price. The Emperor had already shaken the Elector of Brandenburg's loyalty by confirming him in his possession of Pomerania and Schleswig-Holstein. Thanks to him, too, a Hohenzollern was grand master of the Teutonic knights.

At Augsburg he redoubled his efforts. The Fugger bank gave him the means of going one better than the French king, whose representative was powerless to prevent the Elector of Brandenburg, the Archbishop of Cologne, the Count Palatine and the King of Poland (who exercised Bohemia's vote) from passing over into the opposing camp. The Archbishop of Mainz defected in his turn. He gained on two counts, for the Curia had just given him a cardinal's hat to get his support for its policy. On 27 August the Emperor concluded an agreement in favour of Charles with Mainz, Cologne, Brandenburg and the Palatinate.

The Elector of Saxony kept aloof from this bargaining. He was not for sale: his integrity assured him of considerable prestige, and besides he was not on the best of terms with the Emperor. Maximilian had told his counsellor Pfeffinger that there was good in Luther and that he was clever at putting priests down. The Elector would therefore be wise to take care of Luther who might perhaps come in handy one day.

For the Legate the agreement of 27 August was a severe setback. Rome would not forgive him for not having foiled the Emperor's manoeuvre. Troubles never come singly and he learned at the same time that the Diet had refused categorically to vote the tax for a crusade, invoking the 'grievances of the German nation against the Roman power'. The people were too impoverished, and they considered that a lot of money had already left Germany on the pretext of crusades and indulgences. Appropriations were always being imposed on the occasion of ecclesiastical nominations. Pamphlets were circulating which explained that the Pope collected more money in his state than any Christian prince. 'We buy him palliums, we send him asses laden with gold, we exchange our gold for the lead of his bulls. . . . Under the pretext of indulgences, we let ourselves be bled white.'

Despite all this, everyone could see the weakness of the agreement: until the new emperor had been formally elected, the electoral votes would continue to go to the highest bidder. In such a small group, one vote would be enough to change the majority; so it was still in the interests of the Holy See to try to form a bloc capable of tipping the scales to the 'right' side when the time came.

It seemed that the Archbishop of Trier could be counted on. He needed France and had remained loyal to the candidacy of Francis I. The cornerstone of this policy would have to be the Elector of Saxony. From the outset his reputation assured him of superiority over all the other electors. When there was a vacancy on the throne, it was he who assumed the title of imperial Vicar and headed the government throughout the interregnum. He could even be put forward against Charles of Spain as an effective candidate for the crown. In short, in the Legate's eyes, Frederick the Wise became overnight a man to treat with respect, and the Curia soon shared this conviction.

The Prince was perfectly well aware of the advantage which Maximilian's policy had given him. Rome was for the time being in a weak position; it was now or never if he was to intervene in the Luther affair. Frederick's idea was to exploit Cajetan's good feelings towards him and make him take control of the proceedings. Luther wanted impartial judges sitting in Germany. It would be enough to change the summons to Rome into a summons to Augsburg and to replace the judges who were clearly suspect with the Pope's personal representative. Cajetan's character led one to hope that he would perceive things at a deeper level than the mediocre Prierias. The 'prince of Thomists' was better prepared than anyone to enter into dialogue with Luther without letting himself be carried away by anger. And as he needed the Elector of Saxony, he could be relied on to do everything possible to arrange something.

Cajetan agreed eagerly to the audience requested by the Prince. The interview at first dealt with political questions. The request about Luther took the Legate aback. Frederick suggested that his Eminence should question Brother Martin as a father, not as a judge, and leave him free to depart afterwards. It was advisable to refer it to Rome. But the messenger bearing the arrest warrant was approaching Augsburg. . . .

Frederick breathed again. No one could say that he had not listened to the injunction from Rome. He had given the official reply expected of him.

Cajetan soon let it be known that the request was granted. Rome entrusted to the Legate the task of settling everything. He would carefully question Luther, but they were not to discuss matters as equals, nor was the question of papal authority to be raised. The instructions previously given were not revoked – Cajetan was careful, one can be sure, to insist on this. In his heart, he was confident. The plea of the Prince and his secretary Spalatin on Luther's behalf had impressed him. The Wittenberg monk was not a common agitator, but a man filled with sincere ardour.

The desire to gratify the Elector was so great at the Curia that they were not content with this. Frederick was accorded the distinction which he had long coveted: the Golden Rose, blessed and scented – the Holy See's recognition of the virtue of a Christian prince. This was clearly a matter of politics, for another favour granted at the same time was the legitimization of the natural children of the 'virtuous' sovereign, who was not even married.

Luther profited considerably from these intrigues: he was no longer pressed for time, the Roman tribunal was removed from his case, and he was assured of his freedom whatever happened. The Curia's instruction to the Legate certainly did not go as far as that. But Cajetan had no choice: he had to submit to the Elector's will and abide by the terms of the agreement concluded with him.

9
Cajetan

State secrets are not common knowledge outside the sphere of government. In his ignorance of what was planned at Augsburg, Luther met the situation as best he could. He had settled his fate in publishing Prierias' *Dialogue*, together with a summary refutation, scorning to take trouble over an opponent who treated him as if he were a mad dog or had the plague, and who had told Luther quite frankly that if the Pope had given him a bishopric, he would be less fastidious about the abuse of indulgences. Public opinion would judge. The first edition immediately went out of print: Tetzel's party bought all the copies they could lay their hands on, perhaps to provide themselves with arguments, or in any event to limit circulation. Luther also had the sermon on the Ban published, as the only way of getting rid of the forgeries circulating under his name.

On 1 September he made clear his position for Staupitz's sake. Nothing would turn him back from the quest he had undertaken for some years with Staupitz's encouragement, a quest to rediscover true Christianity behind the untruths of the last few centuries. The summons which required him to leave for Rome under pain of excommunication, even the threat of penalties, was nothing.

He had known for a long time, as Staupitz was aware, the kind of inward proof which carries conviction. The difference between what he read in the Bible and the official doctrine of the Church worried him day and night. If Roman authority excommunicated him, his sole fear would be that Staupitz also might condemn him. For he had complete confidence in the judgement of his superior. He at least was a man of God.

If Prierias should again act contemptuously, Luther would not hold himself back. He would show these Romans who thought they were better than others, that no one in Germany was fooled by their cunning. They would try to take truth by the nose, stifle it, and prevent all discussion.

'Pray God that I do not take too much delight and am not too sure of myself in this trial. For my part, I pray God that they should not bear a grudge. I freely admit that they too are filled with sincere zeal; but their zeal is ill-informed and it is a long time since they were enlightened by Christ, our only light.'

Some days later he was encouraged by the humanist Capito from Basle who told him that Erasmus was continually praising his theses. They advised him to adopt the humanist tactic of not clashing head-on with Rome in order to survive more effectively.

It was only on 5 September that a letter from Spalatin informed him of the latest developments. Spalatin had accompanied the Elector on his visit to the Legate and both of them returned favourably impressed. It had been an extended interview. The Cardinal was the kind of man with whom one could talk, and he was not so hostile to Luther that he tried to prejudice the Emperor against him. His cordiality gave rise to hopes that he would manage his task in a gentle and tolerant way. In the end, only Tetzel's party, consisting of ignorant men, declared Luther heretical. The Prince shelved the cunning idea of refusing a safe-conduct: he had another solution.

Clearly, Spalatin knew more than he was letting on. He did not disclose the terms of the agreement with Cajetan to Luther, who must take the hint that everything was going to be all right. What followed showed that there was already a possibility of making him a bishop. On this subject, Spalatin just said: 'Be prudent. If you don't make any false moves, you will have an unexpected opportunity to teach your views.' He assured Luther that he had a great number of admirers. Many people, and Staupitz above all, were doing everything to save his neck, his freedom, and his reputation, and to preserve his chair of Holy Scripture. They hoped he would not do anything foolish.

His sermon on the Ban was a great mistake, and its publication must be prevented at all costs.

The notice arrived too late. Luther had clearly made a tactical error, though unintentionally. In other circles, his revolutionary explanations on excommunication were approved by so many competent persons that he was not sorry to make them available to a larger public.

He had to wait for several days before he could tell Lang, his immediate superior who lived in Erfurt, that he was no longer under the threat of a Roman ultimatum. The Elector had persuaded the Legate to ask for the transfer of the case to Germany. Luther was told to await Rome's reply; but for the moment the threat of sanctions was averted.

The trial would have been only incidental. The main point was still what Luther called 'his' theology. He made fun of the disapproval of the Erfurt masters. 'I am quite happy that your theologians should continue to be shocked by me provided that they let me follow my way. As for their theology, I don't want a bar of it, anywhere or in any way.'

Cajetan had just received an order from Rome that Luther should go to Augsburg, and the Elector lost no time in passing this on. Luther should leave immediately and stop at Weimar to receive instructions. He was not yet at the end of his difficulties. He was being sent to confront in person a man who he knew disapproved of his sermon on excommunication and was, moreover, a Thomist.

Luther was soon on the road, with Brother Leonard Beyer, who had gone with him to Heidelberg, as a companion. He was troubled by gloomy forebodings. The flames of the fire which was possibly awaiting him danced madly in his imagination. The Elector who was casting him into the lion's mouth would certainly not raise an army to rescue him. He worried also about the fate of his kinsfolk. for an executed heretic's family was doomed to shame, discredit and misery.

On 29 September at Weimar, he preached before the Elector

and his court. Frederick had chosen to leave Augsburg, not wanting to find himself between the devil and the deep blue sea. He even refused to receive Luther in private. It was Spalatin who sent him his papers and a little money. Two Saxon lawyers, the counsellors Ruhel and von Feilitzch, were waiting for him at Augsburg. They would see to it that everything turned out well.

Moving from monastery to monastery, they approached Augsburg. Luther was so exhausted that they found a cart in which he could travel the last few kilometres. Everyone everywhere advised him to return home. But he put himself under the protection of Christ 'who reigns even in Augsburg'. He had no choice: if he was not condemned by men, he would be by God.

As soon as he had arrived, he informed the Legate. His Saxon advisers would not let him put a foot outside before obtaining for him an imperial safe-conduct. No one wanted to rely on the Legate's allowing him to leave if the interview turned out badly. Cajetan was, in practical terms, master of the situation. The Diet had ended long since, and the Emperor had left to go hunting. Even the Bishop of Augsburg had preferred to leave the field open for the formidable papal representative.

Luther was hemmed in entirely. Everyone wanted to see the new Herostratus who had set fire to the old world, even Doctor Peutinger, the most famous man in the city. He was known to be under the protection of the Prince of Saxony, and he let Spalatin know that he was conscious of the benefits of this protection.

Among the visitors was Doctor John Eck. In spite of their rather sour writings of the spring, Luther and Eck welcomed each other. Eck had a special grudge against Karlstadt who was implacably against him. Luther offered his good offices: why not settle the quarrel in a good theological disputation? The suggestion was accepted in principle and Luther was given the task of convincing his irascible Wittenberg colleague.

Every day a messenger from the Legate came to fetch the

defendant and was shown the door. Unable to tolerate this any longer, Cajetan sent one of the dignitaries of his own entourage. The man, an Italian, Urban of Serralonga, was to put Luther in his place. He proposed to him point-blank that he should yield without more ado, return to the Church and revoke his statements. Had not the abbot, Joachim of Fiore, long ago avoided being personally condemned as a heretic although his ideas were condemned?

It was a significant manoeuvre. The target was not Luther but his doctrine. If he denied it, he would easily save his neck. There could be no better proof that the stakes in this confrontation were solely doctrinal. That was also his opinion. The prospect of perishing in the defence of views for which he was still fighting alone did not disturb him.

Serralonga tried another approach: 'All the same, you are not going to try to prove your theories. This isn't a tournament.'

'If it can be shown that I have said something other than what the Holy Roman Church believes, I will be the first to condemn myself and recognize my defeat.'

That then was the issue. If Catejan wanted to make the speculation of St Thomas pass for the doctrine of the Church, Luther would revoke nothing. Alternatively the Church would have to deny the teaching of which Luther himself made use.

'Come, come,' replied the other, 'you mustn't take indulgences so seriously. Even if everything that is said isn't true, it brings in the money. Papal power is not a matter for discussion; it is so great that the Holy Father can annul everything he wishes with a nod of his head, even in matters of faith. The Pope is not afraid of the Germans. Do you think that the Prince of Saxony is going to take up arms on your account?'

'Certainly not.'

'Then where will you go?'

'Under heaven.'

Luther concluded by showing the mediator the door. Not much reassured, he nevertheless felt his confidence returning. Apart from the imperial safe-conduct he was expecting

Staupitz's arrival. The Vicar-general would be welcome to take a leading part in an affair which promised to be lively.

At all events, Luther, through Spalatin, took his leave of Wittenberg. The Saxon lawyers had decided that if the cardinal used force, there would be an appeal to a council. But by then God alone knew what could have happened! On Monday the 11th, Luther wrote to the young Philip Melanchthon who had just begun his brilliant professorial career at Wittenberg.

'Take care of the young. I will be burned if God wills, for you and for them. I prefer to die and, what for me is the worst of all, to be deprived of your precious company for ever, rather than to revoke what I have said, which is good. That would be the end of our University and of the excellent studies that can be done there. Don't count on my presence.'

'Italy is plunged into darkness by a gang of fools who are bent on attacking thought and learning. They are incapable of knowing Christ and what is from Christ, but they are masters of our conduct and of our faith. The Lord has truly said: "I will give them children as rulers and the weak ones will have power over them."'

Early next morning the accused, escorted by some monks, finally appeared before Cajetan. In keeping with the ceremonial taught to him, Luther began by prostrating himself on the ground. Then he straightened up and waited on his knees for the cardinal's signal for him to stand up. A throng of curious men, mostly Italians, crowded around the Legate.

Luther apologised for having taken his time to assure himself of imperial protection. He had only done it, he said, at the insistence of friends. He started the ball rolling by declaring to his eminent interviewer that he had come to receive the truth from his own lips.

The cardinal smiled, sure of his duty. He proved cordial and pleasant, as only an Italian can be, with just a hint of friendliness. He had used his enforced sojourn in Augsburg after the Diet profitably by giving close attention to Luther's text on indulgences. The Saxon monk's position seemed to him acceptable on the whole, though a little strained in parts. But the abuses which Luther quite rightly denounced were not sufficient reason to suppress a practice which was centuries old and theologically justifiable. One could therefore dispense with details. The indulgence was not the real question. Luther must make an act of submission and that would be the end of it.

'My son, the Holy Father requests you, before everything else, to repent and retract your errors. You must promise to teach them no longer and to refrain from everything which would be likely to disturb the peace of the Church.'

'Most reverend Father, if I am to retract my errors and be aware of those which I must avoid, they must first be pointed out to me. What are they?'

'You deny that the treasury of indulgences is established by the merits of Christ and the saints. Now, Pope Clement VI has defined this doctrine as a doctrine of faith. Elsewhere, you teach that it is faith, not the sacrament, which justifies. This is a new and false doctrine.'

These were the two closely considered points on which the Legate had decided to conduct the contest. The first allowed him to put the question of papal authority. The second rested on the Thomist doctrine of the sacrament.

Luther retorted unhesitatingly that it was impossible for him to define in any other way the relationship between faith and the sacrament.

'You will retract this thesis, and you will do it this very day!' exclaimed the Legate, amidst the jeering of his supporters. 'If not I condemn everything you have ever said.'

'Furthermore,' Luther calmly continued, 'I recognize no authority in papal decretals. They cite Scripture improperly, and distort the texts from their true sense in order to prove what has already been found in Thomas Aquinas. The Scripture passages quoted in my theses have a superior value.'

'The Pope is above the Council and the Scripture. Did not Nicholas V condemn the Council of Basle? Your assertions have already been condemned in the case of Gerson and his associates.'

'But has not the University of Paris just appealed against the Pope to the next Council?'

'The Parisians are always too hasty!'

The discussion continued in this tone. Cajetan had instructions not to enter into debate with the heretic, but the theologian in him got the better of the judge, though he rigorously conceded nothing to Luther. He derided the latter's quotations of Scripture and repeated incessantly, 'Retract, recognize your error, the Pope requires it.' Or again, 'Do you believe, yes or no?'

Seeing that they were getting nowhere, Luther put an end to the interview by asking permission to retire for reflection.

Such was the disquiet among his supporters that the next day he came back, accompanied by the Saxon lawyers, Staupitz the Vicar-general, and the renowned Peutinger. The Legate just smiled on seeing this imposing body. But his composure was quickly given a sharp jolt. For Luther has also brought a notary with him, and he began by reading in a loud voice a solemn declaration; unless he could be refuted, no one could oblige him to retract; he could not recall having taught anything at all against the Bible, the Church Fathers, the decretals or reason. He was capable of making mistakes like anyone else, and he put himself in this respect under the judgement of the Church. He asked for a public discussion of his theses in Augsburg or somewhere else. If the Legate did not agree, he was ready to reply in writing to the objections which had been made the day before, and to submit his reply to the Universities of Basle, Freiburg, Louvain, and even Paris if necessary.

Cajetan was clearly not inclined to listen to such proposals. His mission was to hush up the affair to please the Elector of Saxony, not to give it still more publicity. Since Luther himself was asking above all to be refuted, he patiently took up again his proof relating to the decretal of Clement VI.

But Luther interrupted him: 'We have fenced enough on this point. I will reply no more except in writing.'

'My son, I have not crossed swords with you, and have no intention of doing so. I am here to listen to you in a fatherly way, to speak the truth to you and, if you wish, to reconcile you with the Holy Father and the Church.'

Staupitz intervened, with the support of Luther's companions; why refuse a written justification? The Legate realised that he must avoid making any false step in front of witnesses who had such powerful connections. He yielded to pressure, but only after stipulating that the text in question would have no juridical value. This was not the answer called for by Luther, but he had had enough and hurried off to draft his defence.

Luther came back before his judge, for the third day running. Once more Ruhel and von Feilitzsch were with him ready to deal with every contingency. The dispute must not be prolonged, and the cardinal must not fail to keep his promise to the prince.

Cajetan took up Luther's paper with a disdainful gesture, and scarcely glanced at it. He promised to send it to Rome. Then he cried out in a tone which brooked no contradiction:

'Retract!'

Putting everything he had into it, he unleashed on Luther a torrent of words. Every time the monk tried to interrupt him, he only shouted more loudly. Luther couldn't get a word in. He had to undergo a course in Thomism, from which the prelate expected a total victory.

But he succeeded only in irritating the Saxon whose greatest virtue was not patience. Luther forgot himself to the point of insulting his judge. And losing all self-control, he declared that, if Clement's text said that the merits of Christ constituted the treasury of indulgences, he would retract everything that was requested.

Taking him at his word, Cajetan grabbed one of the massive tomes from his library, and read from it, without pausing for breath, in the end finding the passage he was looking for.

'Here! Listen: "Christ has acquired a treasure by his passion for the benefit of the Church militant".'

'Alas, most reverend Father, what does this text mean, if not that Christ has acquired a treasure *by* his merits? The merits are not the treasure, but they have made it possible to acquire the remission of sins. There is no other treasure.'

The distinguished theologian showed that the point had hit home, and he tried to cover his embarrassment by passing on to other matters. But Luther had had enough.

'You must not imagine, most reverend Father, that we Germans are also ignorant of grammar.'

Clearly thrown off his course, the cardinal tried again to argue that the Bible itself can be mistaken, since St Matthew attributes to Zachariah a text from Jeremiah. But he stopped in time, before this desperate effort could lead to his own undoing. Finally returning to the only thing which he had to say, he called on Luther for the last time to retract.

'The Pope has given me the power to excommunicate you, as well as those who support you. I can equally well place an interdict on every place where you go.'

The threat fell on deaf ears. Luther didn't care a fig for excommunication or an interdict.

As he made to leave, the cardinal got up and snapped at him. 'Go away and don't come before me again except to retract!'

Though he was more of an intellectual than a diplomat (he had shown this all along), Cajetan was careful not to make the situation any worse. Having eaten, he shut himself up for many hours with Serralonga, Staupitz and another monk, Wenceslas Link, a close friend of Luther. He hoped that the Vicar-general could persuade the obstinate Luther. In this small group he declared that Luther had no better friend than him, and he was sincere. His intelligence enabled him to see the difference between the 'little monk' and his persecutors. In a way, he would like Luther to make it possible for him to vouch for him at Rome. An act of submission would suffice.

The tragedy was that Luther believed that he could not make

the gesture expected of him without denying the convictions he held more dear than life itself. The only way out of the predicament which he could see was for Rome to acknowledge the ideas which he had found in Scripture. That was what Staupitz tried to make the Legate understand. Worried by Cajetan passing on a responsibility whose pitfalls he recognized only too well, he returned the ball into the Legate's court. Luther was too clever for him, he said, only the Legate could get to the bottom of it. The cardinal promised to draw up a list of articles to be retracted. But he did not want to re-examine the monk, whose piercing eyes and strange ideas put him off balance.

Luther, for his part, had lost all confidence in the judge for whom he had asked. To get the case away from him, he was thinking of appealing to the Pope himself. He could not retract a single syllable. If the Legate went on as he had started, Luther would publish the text which he had sent him, so that the whole world could know what it was about. He wrote to Wittenberg that Catejan was a good Thomist, but lacked a clear vision of Christianity. He was as well qualified to hear this case as an ass was to play a harp.

Meanwhile the prelate was disturbed by the text sent back to him, the first part of which dealt with the 'treasury' of indulgences. Luther could not believe that the Pope could dispose at will of the merits of Christ. Clement VI had gone a long way to claim such a power, on the basis of flimsy reasoning. But if the Pope was mistaken, this was serious. The thesis for which he had been accused by Cajetan only underlined Luther's difficulty in getting out of his dilemma: either to admit his own error or to consider that the Pope was mistaken.

The only solution was to admit the Pope's error. Only teachings which conformed to Scripture and tradition were infallible. St Peter himself had had to be led back by St Paul to the truth of the Gospel. And he had submitted one of his decisions for the approval of James and the whole Church. The popes, moreover, often contradicted their predecessors' decrees. A great jurist like Panormitanus declared that in matters of faith it was not only the General Council which was above the pope but every believer who depended on the better texts of the Old and New Testaments.

At the very least, Clement VI's decree led to confusion. It was not illegitimate, therefore, to extract from it one thesis for discussion, as Luther had done in his writings on indulgences. If the present pope could clarify this point, Luther was ready to obey.

The second part of the 'notorious heretic's' apologia had to do with faith: no one could be justified except by faith, so no one should doubt that he was justified, under pain of losing grace. It was on account of this doctrine that Luther was accused of introducing novelties and errors into the Church.

His reply was that no one was righteous except the man who believed in God. This was the one infallible truth. Faith consisted in believing what God promised or said; the Word and Faith were inseparable. The Sacrament was a response of God to the man who asked for grace. Peter Lombard said that it was instituted to fulfil and actualize faith. The Scripture, in a word, proposed nothing else but faith. The numerous texts which Luther cited required him, he declared, to maintain his point of view.

He also begged the cardinal to have pity on him, for conscience's sake; to show him how to understand the Bible otherwise than he did, or to give up urging upon him an impossible retraction. He asked him further to intercede with the Pope. Luther sought only light and truth. He was ready to yield, to change, to recant everything which was shown to be contrary to a better understanding of Scripture. He was not so arrogant or full of his own glory that he would be ashamed to recant. On the contrary, he would be very happy to see truth win.

This exhibition and this moving plea did not leave the Legate indifferent. He would send Leo X a rough draft for a decree on indulgences. And, conscious of the aspects relating to the Thomist doctrine of the sacraments, he told Link, in another interview, that he would no longer press Luther on the matter of faith. He would be content with a retraction of the thesis on the treasury of indulgences. It was the least that he could insist on. But it was also the whole question. Cajetan could not go to Rome empty-handed and Luther believed that it was up to Rome to explain itself. At any rate, the Legate announced, he would not pronounce excommunication immediately. He would first refer the matter to the Curia. The truth was that he preferred to send the case back to its first judges, thus implicitly recognizing the failure of his mission.

His apparently favourable disposition persuaded Staupitz to ask Luther to see if indeed he could not retract, and he begged him to write Cajetan a letter excusing himself for his behaviour in the preceding days. Luther willingly sent the letter, but remained unbending.

The Legate had not concealed from the Vicar-general that the Roman superior of the Augustinian order had given strict orders. Peutinger suspected that it was a question of stopping not only Luther but Staupitz himself. That brought on a state of panic. Staupitz decided that Luther was no longer safe in Germany. He tried to borrow money so that he could take refuge abroad, in France. He went as far as giving him his freedom and releasing him from his vow of obedience. Then he faded out of the picture.

Luther was alone, quite alone. As far as he was concerned, he would let events take their course. He was not seeking to win his case. He was simply waiting for the Church to take up the question he had raised. Determined to follow his conscience alone, he found the arguments of St Thomas and the theologians inadequate. He hoped someone could find better conclusions than his own from the Scriptures, in which case he would immediately give way. For he did not believe that the voice of Christ could be heard except through the voice of the Church.

Days passed without anything more being heard of the Legate. The Elector of Saxony's men in the end became worried, for this silence boded ill. It became a matter of urgency to get

Luther to a safe place. Legally, after the failure of the Elector's manoeuvre the monk was no longer covered by the cardinal's word. The case must automatically revert to the Roman tribunal and, against this, the only appeal was to the Pope in person. But the Pope must not put it in the hands of the same judges. The idea was hatched of distinguishing between the Pope 'misinformed' and the Pope 'better informed'. An appeal would be made from the former to the latter.

The appeal was drafted in the proper form and lodged by a notary in the presence of two witnesses. It asserted the partiality and ignorance of the judges named up to that point, and asked for well-informed papal commissioners sitting in a safer place than Rome, where the Pope himself had almost given in to an uprising of the Curia. Luther's health, moreover, would not allow him to undertake a long journey.

The document was posted on the doors of the Augsburg churches, but before this Brother Beyer had taken it to the Legate – all of this, naturally, after Luther's departure. For there was not a moment to be lost in getting away from a town which threatened to become a trap at any moment.

Reliable friends managed to open one of the city gates for him at night. A horseman was waiting with a second steed. He mounted as he was, in his cassock, without spurs, and the two men rode off at a gallop.

Before disappearing, Luther had left a letter for Cajetan in which he made the point about his legal position: he had appeared, since he had been ordered to do so, and he had done so despite obstacles; he had sent the Pope the essential text around which the debate revolved. Having no more to do at Augsburg, since the Legate had forbidden him to appear before him again, and being short of money, he thought it justifiable to leave. His appeal to the Pope would suit his Eminence, for it was said that this case weighed heavily on him. It had been done in full accord with the Elector of Saxony, who preferred this solution to a retraction. As to this last point, the Legate would understand Luther's position. Many people were of the opinion that to retract assertions whose falsity one did not understand was to run the risk of not knowing truth or error any more. It was for the Church to condemn error and not for a particular person to decide about it.

Cajetan was dumbfounded. What could he say to Rome and to the Elector? He had obtained no result; he had let the two suspects, Luther and Staupitz, escape. Luther had been very careful not to tell him where he was going. Things were back to where they had started. He informed Rome that, having done all that he could, he was declining all responsibility from now on. On 25 October, to justify himself in Frederick's eyes, he drew up a report of the case, in which he began by reproaching the prince for obtaining for Luther an imperial safe-conduct. He insisted on the great good will of which he had given proof and gave a detailed account of the three interviews. Luther's arguments had been completely beside the point. He had dared to attack the Pope by claiming that the decretals made a false use of Scripture. His obstinacy and deceit were beyond belief. What could be impelling him to such obstinacy? To conclude, the Legate stated his findings:

1. Luther would have us believe that his original theses were only theses for discussion. But his other publications were positive assertions. Among his ideas, some were contrary to the doctrine of the Holy apostolic see, others purely and simply worthy of condemnation. Cajetan added that he said this with full knowledge of the case, and there was no doubt that it was he who understood the whole matter best.

2. I exhort your Highness and beg you in the interests of honour and conscience, either to send Luther to Rome or to expel him from your territory.

3. A matter so serious and injurious should not drag out any longer. Rome will take control of the matter and follow it through to its conclusion.

Before sending this letter, Cajetan waited for other news – perhaps, in fact, for authorization to write in this way to the Elector. Towards the middle of November the document, copied by scribes, finally left for Wittenberg, with a postscript in the cardinal's own hand. 'I beg and abjure your Highness not to be led into error by those who declare that what Brother Martin has said contains nothing reprehensible. Do not blemish the glory of your ancestors for the sake of a miserable monk. Recall your repeated promises. What I say is nothing but the unvarnished truth.'

10
Farewell to Wittenberg

On the eve of All Saints' Day Luther returned safe and sound to Wittenberg. But how long could he remain there? A year had passed since his letter to the Archbishop of Mainz and he was no more than a fugitive. A messenger from Spalatin had brought him in Nuremberg a copy of the letter of 23 August which ordered his immediate arrest: the Elector had managed to obtain the fateful document through his spies in the Legate's entourage. An official intimation of the Pope's wishes was expected at any moment.

The traveller had only just arrived when he found a messenger about to leave for the prince's court. There was no time to give a detailed account of the events of Augsburg. Luther contented himself with hastily dictating some news and some impressions.

He had appealed to the Pope. If the sovereign pontiff rejected his appeal by virtue of his supreme discretionary power, the only option he had left would be to follow the lead of the University of Paris and appeal to the next Council.

Luther felt full of joy and peace. He was astonished that so many men in high places considered his case so seriously. The Legate had kept his promise to treat him generously. But there had been a bit of sharp practice. There was no doubt of Cajetan's sincerity. but he had determined beforehand not to budge if Luther refused to retract, and that was where the conflict lay. Finally, it seemed that Rome's orders had been to condemn Luther, not to reach a correct judgement. The only thing to do now was to publish the proceedings of the pseudo-trial and appeal to a 'better-informed pope'.

How could anyone believe that the letter of arrest had originated with the sovereign pontiff? Leo X was not the sort to condemn a man without hearing him, without even waiting for the tribunal's period of grace to run out. The forger who believed he could intimidate Luther would soon find out that no one was fooled, for Luther would publish an analysis of the document. And if indeed the Roman Curia was at the bottom of this atrocity, it would recognise its own stupidity and learn not to go too far. Though the cardinal had appeared very sure of himself, Rome, it seemed, was beginning to have doubts about its case and was trying to extricate itself from its own false move.

On 19 November the Elector showed Luther the official report of the interview at Augsburg which he had just received from the Legate. Before replying to the cardinal, he asked Luther to give his own version of the events. Luther seized this opportunity to clarify his position. It was also important to feed the prince arguments with which he could effectively resist the pressures being brought to bear on him. He would report everything in detail, reply to all of Cajetan's assertions and examine all the assumptions.

The Legate, he began, should not blame the Elector for the safe-conduct. His Highness had shown his confidence in the cardinal's word by letting Luther leave for Augsburg. Nor did the responsibility rest with Luther himself, but with the eminent men who surrounded him with their advice. They were all Germans and a German could be excused for preferring the unanimous advice of his fellow-countrymen to the contrary opinion put forward by the Italian Serralonga.

Luther had assured the Legate that he had been only too ready (as he still was) to submit to a doctrine better than his own. But Catejan had replied that the Pope had ordered him to obtain a retraction, without ever showing the letter containing such instructions.

As regards the errors attributed to Luther, Cajetan had first mentioned a phrase taken from the explanation of the seventh thesis on indulgences. 'He who receives the sacrament (of penance) must believe that he will unquestionably receive sacramental grace.' This proposition was contrary to Holy Scripture and to the teaching of the Church. Luther had then explained that he would never yield on this point, for he was backed by a great number of Scriptural texts. The cardinal, though he said he would invoke only the Bible and official texts and not the opinions of theologians, had been unable to produce a single syllable of Scripture to support his objection. He was able only to cite texts of councils relating to the efficacy of the sacraments, texts which Luther did not deny and which proved nothing against him.

Today again he begged to be shown a single passage of Scripture or of the Church Fathers which contradicted his statement. He was so concerned that he called on the prince himself to be his witness: 'I regret with all my being that this precept of faith should be considered doubtful, new, or even false. Before God and his angels, I accept my defeat on the treasury of indulgences issue. But I will maintain to death my idea of faith. I will deny everything else rather than retract on this point, for that would be to deny Christ himself; unless, of course, I am shown the opposite by Scripture, which has not yet been done, and if God please, will never be done.'

But Catejan himself said that the indulgences issue mattered more than that of faith. And on this subject he claimed that Luther's arguments against Clement VI's decree were beside the point. But in saying this he was taking advantage of the prince's ignorance of theology. For Luther's argument amounted to saying that, while the text in question called on the Scriptures for its support, it distorted their meaning. Cajetan could not bear the Pope being accused of distorting the Bible: he wished the Pope's statements to be accepted without questioning whether they conformed to the Scripture or not. But to take only one example, didn't another papal text say that the priesthood of Christ had been transferred to St Peter . . . so that he became a giver of law in his own right? And as a basis for this, the epistle to the Hebrews was quoted: 'As the priesthood has been transferred, it is necessary that the law – the legislative power – be also transferred.' Are the priesthood and the law of Christ thus abrogated for St Peter's benefit? It would be very troublesome to escape from the impious conclusion of such reasoning. Canon law contained many proofs of the same kind, and by these errors Scripture was obscured if not corrupted. This was especially true of the text relating to the treasury of indulgences. Christ's merits could not be handed out by men and the Scripture called for penance rather than doing without it by acquiring indulgences. The Church's practice was not a traditional custom, as was asserted, but an abuse and corruption of Scriptural truth. 'The decree of Clement VI is true, I concede, but his meaning is not that of the Scriptural texts on which it rests. They were in existence centuries before him, and it wasn't necessary to wait this long to recognize their meaning.

'I am asked to accept the canonical sense and to reject the Scriptural sense. I respect human declarations, but I cannot be asked to deny the Word of God. If a man declares that the Pope and the Fathers have sometimes distorted Scripture, this cannot be described as nonsense unless a decision has been made in advance to condemn him without a hearing.'

In short, there was no point in discussing it. The Legate wanted Luther to accept everything he said and he refused to listen. He even scoffed at his Scriptural quotations, urging that the Pope was superior to Scripture and to the Council. The only choice Luther had was between retraction and condemnation. Since Cajetan would not allow any discussion, the only course open to him was to make a written reply which could be examined by others and which would prevent the cardinal from telling just any story he liked. Cajetan had not even taken up the request for Luther's doctrine to be examined by the Holy Father or the universities. He claimed that his role was to reconcile Luther with the Church as if the latter had already been legally declared a heretic, an apostate shut out from the community of the Church.

Staupitz had only with great difficulty persuaded Cajetan to accept his written reply. He was clearly ready to make a settlement, but only after Luther had recanted. Luther's document drew only contemptuous comments from the Legate; he saw in it nothing but verbiage, and said that Luther's Scriptural quotations were irrelevant; moreover, he had given them their true interpretation. This had not prevented him from joining in on the discussion on the words: Christ 'has acquired'. Finally, when he sent Luther off he forbade him to come back unless to retract. So Cajetan had done nothing but confirm Luther's conviction that he must not retract until he had been convinced of his errors. Luther had given the same answer to Staupitz who tried, for the Legate's sake, to make him give in. 'Can you explain to me what else my Scripture texts mean?' 'No, it is beyond my powers.' 'Well then, my conscience forbids me to retract unless someone explains the Bible otherwise than I understand it.' Altogether Luther felt he had done all he could to reply, with due obedience, to the papal summons.

To Cajetan's three conclusions he made the following reply: the Legate recognised that the theses on indulgences were only questions; now an action can be brought only on the basis of *conclusions*; despite that, the indictment consisted only of the ninety-five theses. The condemnation, therefore, was entirely gratuitous and arbitrary. The fact that it was linked, after the event, with Luther's sermons in no way validated the indictment. Luther, moreover, would defend the sermons more readily than his theses.

It was curious that Cajetan distinguished, in the sermons, what was 'worthy of condemnation' from what was 'contrary to the doctrine of the Apostolic see': since the accusation rested essentially on a doctrine contrary to the teaching of the Apostolic see, it followed that Luther had said nothing worthy of condemnation!

If only Prierias had been the author of the Legate's letter!

Luther would have enjoyed showing how a bad conscience would be incapable of acting with integrity. But if the respect owing to the person of Cajetan made Luther hold himself back, he could not let the Legate make a new Pilate out of a prince as judicious as his Highness. For the Legate's argument amounted to saying, 'If this man were not guilty, I would not accuse him.' Let him therefore show in writing what his case was. A great prince had no need to listen to the judgement and advice of a little Italian, a Roman.

Luther begged the prince to tell him what more he could have done or what more he could still do. He had answered the summons when all his friends thought that he had not needed to; he had explained himself before the papal Legate. He could have refused to reply since the *Explanations* had been sent directly to the Pope himself. He could not see that he had left out anything at all except those six letters: REVOCO, 'I recant'.

'The Legate, and even the Pope, could interpret, assert, condemn as they please. But let them not say "You are deceived, you are mistaken", without pointing out their objections in writing. Let them show what other meaning they give to my Scriptural texts and not just contend that these texts prove nothing. Let them instruct one who desires, asks, begs, wants, and expects to be enlightened! Even a Turk wouldn't refuse to do it! And if I finally see what other meaning can be drawn from these texts, and still persist and do not retract, let your Highness be the first to persecute me, let the University deny me, let the Lord Jesus himself abandon me!

'If I am too insignificant to be accorded the honour of being taught the truth, perhaps his Eminence would at least deign to tell your Highness in what respect I have erred, and what is the basis for accusing me. It is so strange to be accused of error without being able to know why or in what!

'I am refused the public discussion I asked for, I am refused a private debate or a written explanation of my errors; the judgement of the four universities is rejected in advance. If a request on the part of your Highness is rejected as well, what can be the conclusion except, purely and simply, that someone has a grudge against me?

'For my part, I ask and beg that your Lordship should not believe those who are saying that Brother Martin has spoken evil, without having listened and without having shown him how he has erred. Peter was mistaken even after having received the Holy Spirit. A cardinal, however learned, can also be mistaken.

'Your Highness' honour and conscience forbid you from sending me to Rome. No man can compel you, especially as it would be impossible for me to go there in safety. It would be downright murder; the Pope himself is not safe. And they have paper, pens, ink, and lawyers. What would be easier for them than to put in writing how and why I am in error? It would be less trouble to enlighten me from a distance in writing than to lure me into an ambush to get rid of me.

'It is sad to see that the Legate dares to suggest that I did all this at your Highness' instigation. Sycophants had already spread reports of this about my theses. Now none of my friends, even those closest to me, knew anything about them. At first I only wrote to the Archbishop of Mainz and the Bishop of Brandenburg. It was their place to put down the abuses and I wrote to them privately before publishing my theses. I knew that this concerned the bishops rather than lay princes. My letters are there to prove it and everyone knows that.

'I ask but one thing of your Highness. For me, certainly, but also for sacred truth, for the honour of the Church, the sovereign pontiff and the Legate himself, and again for your Lordship's reputation, let your Highness ask that clarification be given of the reasons and the authorities which indicate that I am in error.

'I have no objection to going into exile. My opponents are everywhere, and I cannot escape them indefinitely. What can a poor monk hope for when an electoral prince of the Holy Roman Empire, whose piety is so outstanding, sees himself threatened by who knows what calamity if he refuses to get rid of me!

'I wish nothing so much as to avoid any trouble for your Highness on my account. I am therefore going to leave this territory to go where God wills. I have no wish to harm anyone. I will everywhere remember your benefits and will pray for you.'

To this long memorandum, written in his own hand, Luther added a letter intended for Spalatin. The prince must at all costs read or have read to him the accused's justification. Luther had tried to strike all the right notes, first of all by showing that Cajetan in many ways treated Frederick in a way a sovereign could not tolerate. He knew that the prince was embarrassed by his presence at Wittenberg, and he had therefore anticipated this difficulty by making clear his decision to go away. But in his heart he hoped that the Elector would ask him to stay. So he spelled out to Spalatin several supplementary arguments which he had not wished to put in a report which was obviously going to be communicated to the Legate. Cajetan, despite his reputation, was a poor theologian. He did not know Scripture and put forward ideas which from anyone else would be considered heretical. In putting at their head such an intellect, and his 'second', Prierias, the Dominicans showed that, among them, no one was worthy to be called a Christian. One could only deplore the time lost by these unfortunate men in studies which had resulted only in ignorance. They had discarded Christ to institute the reign of Aristotle, the worst of the sophists.

Having said this, he had to wait and see if the prince himself would write to the Pope to get the case put finally to German judges. For the condemnation of Luther would open the way to new attacks already in full swing, this time against Karlstadt and the faculty of theology in Wittenberg; and the university would not recover from it. The Dominicans would certainly stop at nothing.

On 23 November the University of Wittenberg joined Luther in asking the prince to obtain from Rome a precise account of what exactly they objected to in one of its professors. It was not easy for the Elector to choose his position: the arrest warrant for Luther was expected at any time, and it would be practically impossible to ignore such an order.

It would be best if the 'notorious heretic' were no longer to be found in the Elector's territory. Luther understood this. Moreover he could not hope to find refuge in another state of the Holy Roman Empire. The Legate would move quickly to find him out. The only place to go to escape from the Roman power was France. The antipapal climate behind the Council of Pisa was still active there, witness the recent appeal of the University of Paris.

Luther spent the rest of November setting his affairs in order. He returned to Spalatin some papers which his friend had passed on to him, including a passionate speech by the Bishop of Liège at the Diet of Augsburg against the conduct of the Roman administration. He gave the printers the *Proceedings* of his interview with Cajetan, after waiting for a long time for the Elector's permission to print. He also thanked Christopher Langenmantel who had helped him in his flight from Augsburg.

As the priest of the principal parish was unwell, Luther was asked to preach in his place. He took the opportunity to say his farewell in veiled words: 'You know that I am a preacher who disappears. How many times have I had to leave you without warning? If that should happen again, I am glad I have had the chance of saying farewell, in case I don't return. Don't let the papal censures with which I am threatend scare you. Don't hold this against anyone, especially not the Holy Father. Trust in God, and bear a grudge against no man. . . .'

He warned Spalatin that he might disappear at any moment. In fact he had already fixed the date of his departure. He would leave one farewell note; but would Spalatin have the courage to read an excommunicate's letter?

The time had now come to appeal from the Pope to a council. It was the last legal manoeuvre left open to him and it brought him into line with the University of Paris whose help and protection he planned to request.

On the 28th at three o'clock in the afternoon, he lodged his appeal before a notary in the church where he had preached the same morning. Scarcely was this ceremony over than a messenger from the prince disclosed that Luther's action met with approval in high places. Nothing else was said. Luther was not detained.

On 1 December in the evening, Luther took leave of his friends in the Augustinian community, assembled for the last time around him. He would leave during the night, after sharing their frugal meal which poverty and sorrow prevented them from turning into an occasion. Some days before they had had to beg the Elector to send them some game so that they could celebrate a new doctor's promotion. Staupitz's efforts to find finance had not been very fruitful. . . .

For the rest of his life, Luther would remember this evening, when he stood face to face with the unknown. Like Abraham, he was ready to go where God would lead. He recalled fearfully his flight from Augsburg, his night ride on a poor mount, tangled up in his robes. . . . At the staging points, unable to hold himself upright, he had collapsed in the stable straw. . . .

They had not even taken their places at the table when a message came from the court. 'Why has Dr Luther not yet departed? There is not a moment to lose.' Luther was distressed. 'My father and mother have abandoned me, but the Lord has taken me to himself,' he said later. Solitude seemed anxious to cover him with her shroud.

But during supper, word came from Spalatin: if Dr Luther has not yet left, let him remain, for his Highness has directions to give him. What had happened? Had the arrest warrant arrived? There were no details. The danger was certainly not over. But there were persistent rumours that the Elector and the University had joined Luther's side. There had recently been discussions with the Bishop of Brandenburg about the support on which Luther could count. Some had suggested that Erasmus, Capito, and other distinguished men of learning would back him; but the Bishop thought these names did not carry sufficient weight to influence the Pope. Only the Elector and the University counted. Now if the relationship between Luther and the University was a factor in his favour, the same was not true of the close relationship between Luther and the Elector. For if the Elector were obliged to give way, Luther, who in any case did not want to compromise him, would be forced to fall into line with him. The prince must claim he is not competent, as a layman, to take up a position in a doctrinal controversy. He could do this much more easily if a University approved by the Church refrained from condemning Luther.

Luther reluctantly agreed to the idea of staying in Wittenberg. He saw himself as already having left and having sacrificed his life. Now he would have to be on the lookout all over again; and he would no longer have the freedom to talk and write. Some even suggested that he would just be a prisoner in the Elector's hands: the Elector would hide him somewhere, and write to the Legate that he was keeping him in a safe place, awaiting an eventual trial.

He was told to meet Spalatin immediately. The interview was to take place in the castle of Lichtenberg near Pretzsch, and had to be kept secret. At Lichtenberg, Luther learned that the Elector was no longer in a hurry to see him leave. Spalatin urged him not to rush off to France. Luther replied that if the condemnation should arrive, he must go immediately. And as he must be able to decide on this flight at any moment, he asked for authorization to publish the *Proceedings* at Augsburg, and his appeal to a council. He had already begun to have this printed without the Elector's permission for which he had been awaiting for some weeks. But this request came up against a brick wall. Spalatin even urged that the sections already printed be destroyed.

Luther had no time to think about how he was going to carry out this instruction, which was in any case difficult to accomplish: for on his return to Wittenberg, he learned that a Roman courtier, Charles Miltitz, had arrived in Germany. This man boasted of having promised the Pope that he would capture the monk and bring him to him; and for this purpose he was armed with letters conferring on him the necessary powers.

This new threat added to Luther's preoccupations: he was not sure whether the censures were still on their way; he might fall any day to an assassin's sword; Miltitz could appear at any moment. But the worst would be if he were brought down one way or another before he could have the *Proceedings* and the appeal printed: he could not let the enemy have a chance of doing away with these documents.

Ignoring the court order, he had the *Proceedings* printed and the appeal to the Council set up in type. The printer would send him the whole edition, which would only be distributed when circumstances allowed. Then he committed himself to Providence. The worse the situation became, the more his courage and resolution increased. His opponents believed that they were nearing the end of their enterprise, but they had seen nothing yet. He was amazed at the ideas which came to his mind and the writings which flowed from his pen: if the occasion offered he would show that the Roman Curia was the kingdom of the Antichrist, of which St Paul spoke. This enemy was much more dangerous than the Turk, about whom the Elector and Spalatin were conferring again with the Legate in the little village of Jena. . . .

Luther took up teaching and preaching again. On 8 December he had given the traditional sermon on the Immaculate Conception. As part of his continuing concern for the University, he had the courses of Thomistic physics and logic abolished; the study of Aristotle's texts was sufficient, especially since Scotist philosophy and logic were still being taught. His struggles for the past two years, were beginning to bear fruit. Luther's master-stroke was to have engineered the appointment of Philip Melanchthon to the chair of Greek. After three weeks teaching, this twenty-year-old master already had an audience of four hundred, including students from all over Germany and Switzerland. The humanists sent their pupils, while mature men left everything to study for a term at the University of Wittenberg which Luther likened to an ant's nest. In fact, it became more and more difficult to find rooms in town, even for a resident.

In pressing the printer to stockpile the texts as they came off the press, Luther had asked the impossible; his work popped up everywhere like mushrooms. The inevitable happened: the instalments were gradually sold as the work proceeded! Luther consoled himself quickly enough, despite his irritation and embarrassment. He sent Link and Staupitz the account which he had drafted for the Elector, as well as a copy of the *Appeal*. But what was the prince going to say?

It wasn't long before he knew. The court had got wind of the publication of the *Proceedings*. Accepting the *fait accompli*, the Elector authorized this text but indicated that the passage which asserted that the letter of 23 August was a forgery would have to be deleted. As for the *Appeal*, the prohibition on publication was maintained.

Relieved at least on one point, Luther still wondered what the prince would decide to do about him. Melanchthon, who was Reuchlin's grand-nephew, suggested that he write to the scholar who had coped for some years with the defenders of orthodoxy. His case was still not ended, but the old humanist had obtained an indefinite papal adjournment.

Luther told Reuchlin of the benefit which his battle had brought all those in Germany who were hoping to study the Bible freely without reference to the scholastic commentaries in which the pure doctrine had been shrouded for centuries. Luther had not been mixed up in the controversy, but he had lost nothing by waiting. For the humanist's opponents were taking revenge for their failure on the man who seemed to more and more people to be Reuchlin's successor. If Luther was less fit to carry the torch, he would, he assured Reuchlin, put as much heart in it. He had nothing to lose because he possessed nothing.

Just as he sent this letter, which was never answered, his long uncertainty was about to be ended. On 20 December, in fact, he learned that the Elector had just notified the Legate that he refused to hand Luther over.

Frederick's silence had been due above all to the complexity of the situation in which Cajetan's ultimatum put him. He had to choose between Luther and the Curia. All of Wittenberg, the University, the Council, were for Luther but Frederick could not afford to tangle with Rome.

As early as 19 November he had written in his own hand to Pfeffinger, ordering him to try a line of action with the Emperor – that his Majesty should intercede with the Holy Father in Luther's favour, since he was an excellent theologian and it would be unjust to put an end to him when he was willing to be shown his errors.

While he was awaiting the outcome, it was wiser to keep Luther at a distance. Cajetan himself suggested it and Luther said that he was ready to leave Wittenberg. The suspect, therefore, would be encouraged to make himself scarce. But just when the prince had sent the order to put this plan into immediate effect, a letter from Pfeffinger made him change his mind. The Curia had just entrusted the affair to a 'commissioner', which suggested that the Legate had been removed from the case. Luther's new judge, who came straight from Rome, had optimistic plans and spoke of coming privately to the Elector before the end of December. Everything suggested that, until then, the monk would be left in peace. If that were so, nothing was urgent, and Spalatin could send out the counter-order which took Luther by surprise.

Following this, Frederick summoned his council. Von Feilitzsch, who had been present at the Augsburg proceedings, had no difficulty in procuring a unanimous decision not to hand Luther over. In his memorandum Luther had given arguments justifying a plea of estoppel and it was enough to repeat it in a letter. As Luther pertinently showed, the Elector had conformed to the order to make Luther appear before the judge chosen by Rome. The Legate's promises had been only a sham: he had urged retraction without himself examining the offence. The University and many knowledgeable men did not see how Luther's doctrine was impious, non-Christian, or heretical; his accusers were clearly interested parties and had never proved what they put forward. There was no need for the Elector to be called upon to do his duty; he had hoped that in the circumstances he would be spared a summons. Luther had still not been convicted of the crime of heresy; handing him over would be to the detriment of the University of Wittenberg, whose competence and orthodoxy no one questioned. Luther's requests to be judged by other universities, and to be allowed to debate his own doctrines, were legitimate; alternatively, his errors must be shown to him in writing. The Elector must know for what reasons he should consider Luther a heretic and deal severely with him; he could not regard as a heretic a man whose guilt had not yet been established.

Spalatin undertook to draft the letter, not without his master putting his hand to it several times. It had to be done quickly, because of the meeting with the Legate at Jena. Moreover, Luther must at all costs refrain from publishing the *Proceedings* of the Augsburg interview and especially his *Appeal* to the Council: that manoeuvre had become pointless, now the means had been found of stopping the Roman proceedings.

The publication of the *Proceedings* meant the worst was to be feared. Luther had to be hidden quickly. The Elector's letter to Cajetan was communicated to him, along with the order that he should not publish his *Appeal*.

But it was too late. Crestfallen, Luther had to admit that he had committed a monumental error. He could only promise not to publish the *Appeal* without consulting the lawyers.

The truth of the matter was that he had been carried away, and he was not slow to heap praises on the letter: the prince knew how to show the Legate, who held his power from men, that one cannot insult with impunity those who hold their authority directly from God.

11

Commissioner Miltitz

After so many weeks of anguish, Luther was to celebrate Christmas peacefully. It was a very relaxed letter which he wrote on the 21st to Spalatin, who wanted to know if war against the Turks could be justified on the basis of the Scriptures. Rome was pressing for a defensive war, as the Turks were advancing towards Hungary and Vienna.

Along with Erasmus, Luther spoke out against the crusade initially, it seems, for the same reasons as the humanist. The great problems of Europe were of no consequence, for it was in man himself that the battlefields worthy of such effort were to be found. What was the point of defeating the Turks if the victors lost the battle for the spirit? Further, the teaching of Scripture was that a religious war without inward conversion was bound to be a failure even militarily.

The enemy of Christianity at the moment was not the Sultan but the Roman Curia; these men, these institutions, these cogwheels who jointly and severally controlled the progress of the Church from Rome. It was really a fiction that it was possible to call it to account without hurting individuals. The Turks menaced the Church only from the outside, while the Curia corrupted the body from the inside. It fought against Christ by making itself out to be more important and necessary than him, while claiming to act in his name.

The clergy wallowed in luxury, greed and ambition, while the Church everywhere presented a miserable face. Such a Church could not lead a good war nor win successful victories. Its principal opponent was God himself, and it was He who must be conquered by tears, sincere prayer, a holy life and a pure faith.

From politics and theology Luther led his correspondent to spirituality, to the battle of the conscience, the centre of gravity of his thoughts. He could be counted on not to 'speak of angels'; that is to say, to develop a comfortable theology which makes an abstraction out of conscience. His watchword was Christ crucified, the mystery of the Cross and of faith in the daily experience of each man.

This deeply ingrained animosity against the Curia was a psychological trait of the Germans at this time. By its abuses the Curia deserved to become a scapegoat, charged with all the sins of the Church. Luther feared it less and less: since the prince had done what was necessary, he would stay in Wittenberg. That was decided. He no longer thought a disaster was imminent.

But the respite was to be short, for soon after Christmas news arrived which seemed to indicate fresh complications. Luther's instinct was right: things were only just beginning.

Counsellor Pfeffinger, who had just reached Saxony, announced the impending arrival of the mysterious Charles Miltitz, the new Roman envoy. Luther soon obtained details, for Pfeffinger forwarded him a letter from the lawyer, Scheurl, one of his friends in Nuremberg.

Scheurl knew Miltitz personally, and had been able to have two days of talks with him, which went on far into the night. He could therefore give Luther all the latest news; and they had talked of nothing but him in these conversations.

In the Curia, Charles Miltitz, a Saxon of the lesser nobility, was private chamberlain to the Pope and a notary; he was fond of the good life and mixed easily with everyone; he had none of the intellectual severity of the learned Cajetan, and he was confident he could settle Luther's case in an amicable fashion. If he had been at Augsburg, things would have gone off altogether differently.

But, of course, Miltitz was, first of all, in the Pope's service, and his loyalty towards his master was absolute. His plan of campaign was flexible, except on one point: the Pope must not be contradicted, but obeyed. In his eyes the most serious item on Luther's dossier was not the list of theses and the *Explanations*, but the sermon in German in which he tried to put the people on their guard against indulgences. Cardinal Accolti, a member of the Curia, found in Luther's sermons more invention than doctrine. . . .

Miltitz undertook to tell the Pope of Tetzel's clever jingle:
'As soon as the coin in the coffer rings
    the soul from Purgatory springs'
which had made the Holy Father furious.

'The idiot! The Pig!' he had shouted.

Prierias was no better off:
'This imbecile who boasts of having drawn up his report in three days would have done better to think about it for three months!'

The master of the Holy Palace was rewarded by a dressing down from the Pope, and everyone turned on him in ridicule.

According to Miltitz, Luther's reply to Prierias made the Pope decide to bring out, towards the middle of November, an official declaration on indulgences, addressed to Cajetan, which the cardinal was instructed to have published in Latin and German.

Miltitz had deposited at Augsburg in the Fuggers' safe deposit, together with the Golden Rose, a voluminous packet of letters some of which were addressed to Prince Frederick. But first he wanted to be sure of the good disposition of the man who would receive them. Though the chamberlain had the rank of apostolic commissioner, he would go to the prince only in his private capacity. Pfeffinger had advised him to do so in the interests of his mission: for the Elector was not a man to be impressed by the Golden Rose or any other favour.

The Pope and Cardinal de Medici had written to Pfeffinger asking him to help the commissioner find a way of settling the Luther case. Pfeffinger was of the opinion that the Pope must be obeyed. If Luther retracted, he could expect to receive a bishopric ... or even more! Nothing displeased the Pope so much as insubordination. Throughout his pontificate he had made a practice of handing out cardinals' hats to those who agreed to bow before him.

Many thought it was pointless for Luther to think of finding refuge in France. King Francis I would not resist a request from Rome for more than three days. This was also the advice of the Emperor who counselled Luther to obey. Besides princes had shown they were little inclined to fight for the Gospel or for truth: at the Council of Pisa in 1511, the King of France and the Emperor did nothing after the cardinals withdrew; and Cardinal Carvajal had to submit, declaring that he thought that he had done no wrong.

Here, therefore, was what Luther anticipated. He was soon going to have to confront a new representative from Rome and the crucial question would face him once again: to yield or not to yield? Would he give in to Scheurl, who advised him not to insist on being tried because he had too little experience of the subtleties of the law? If his conscience impelled him to obey Scripture rather than the Pope, he must remember that in the eyes of many it was the Pope's business to interpret Scripture. It was always best to give in for the time being, and wait for a favourable opportunity.

In examining his conscience once again Luther realised that he was ready to concede everything except the actual matter over which the storm had broken out. It was his duty to ask the ecclesiastical authority to adopt the cause of a religion based on the spirit of the Biblical message. The stir his intervention had provoked, proved that he was right about the seriousness of the problem. Many found the answer to these questions in his writings and Scheurl assured him that, according to Miltitz, the Roman Curia would give a lot to see the end of the conflict. The Curia didn't want to be seen to burn its bridges, but it continued to demand an impossible submission from Luther. Could a man be condemned for having asked that the Pope be a real Pope?

Miltitz's arrival at Altenburg Castle where the Elector lived put an end to the waiting. It was 28 December, the Feast of the Holy Innocents, and at the commissioner's request Frederick ordered Luther to come and see the papal envoy.

At the beginning of January, in obedience to the prince, the monk was face to face with papal authority for the second time in three months. The meeting took place in the home of Spalatin, the canon of Altenburg: so his Holiness's commissioner had escaped from the icy rooms of the ducal fortress!

Miltitz was no ascetic; he loved life and its pleasures. His standing in the Curia was good enough for him to be appointed ambassador of the Golden Rose, and he was well aware of his importance. His ambassadorial status would bring him substantial gratuities. His task was to go through a number of nominations, and it was customary for successful applicants to show their gratitude. The Elector Frederick procured the legitimization of his natural children, who were thereby made eligible for appointment to ecclesiastical positions: another profit in prospect!

Miltitz was even prepared to take advantage of the task which had been added to his chief mission before his departure: for the idea of sending the Golden Rose to obtain the prince's co-operation in the settlement of the Luther case came to the Curia after the Legate's failure at Augsburg. This affair was taking the same course as the Reuchlin case. The Germans had an infernal ability to thwart all legal process; and while they gained time feelings ran high against the Roman Curia and the traditional theologians. Reuchlin's trial had provoked many more defamatory pamphlets, such as the *Letters of Obscure Men*. In just one year, the consequences of Luther's resistance were already proving disastrous.

The Pope approved the plan. Psychologically, he felt closer to Miltitz than to Cajetan, and much closer than to the fumbling Prierias. The chamberlain was a little young, but his twenty-seven years allowed him great flexibility. Besides, he would be subordinate to the Legate who alone would decide what use to make of Miltitz's letters which were aimed at Luther's extradition, and who could even, if circumstances warranted it, cancel the presentation of the Golden Rose.

On his arrival at Augsburg, the commissioner had found Cajetan was at Linz with the Emperor. Left to himself, he accepted Pfeffinger's hospitality, while he waited to leave with him for Saxony. The information which he received during these few weeks had decided him to settle the Luther affair without reference to the Legate. He had been asked just to sound out the Elector of Saxony discreetly, but he determined to be the man with the solution for which everybody was looking. His plan was simple: since the pair responsible for the trouble were Tetzel and Luther, he would summon them to appear and would obtain their silence by intimidation. He thought that he was dealing with two old men and that his status as papal representative would impress them for sure.

Even before meeting Luther, he summoned Tetzel who excused himself, pleading sickness and fear of being attacked on the road by the Lutherans. Miltitz merely suspected deceit. But it would do no harm now to keep Tetzel waiting.

Luther probably benefited from the commissioner's displeasure with the Dominican. His youth, in any case – he was 35 – surprised Miltitz, who had not expected to hold discussions with a man scarcely older than himself. His welcome was more than cordial.

In the presence of the ubiquitous von Feilitzsch, the commissioner announced that he had considered the main points of the complaints raised against Luther: he had seduced the people and given them a false understanding of and a scorn for indulgences. In his favour, Miltitz admitted that Luther had been provoked by Tetzel who, because he was bound to serve the Archbishop of Mainz, for motives of self-interest had gone a great deal too far.

Luther retorted that the Pope carried the most responsibility. He could only blame himself for attacks against the Roman Church. Why had he granted three bishoprics to Albert of

Brandenburg? Even then, why ask so much money for giving what he himself held freely from God? The Bishop, of course, had to find this money and the means was the preaching of indulgences. There again, the Pope let things go on without saying anything, which was why Luther lost patience. He could no longer stand seeing the people exploited and the Florentines taking advantage of the Pope's goodness to gratify a greed as inextinguishable as the fires of hell. The opportunity of at last telling these Roman courtiers the truth was too good to let slip.

Without letting himself be thrown by this attack, Miltitz persuaded Luther to let the controversy die down of its own accord, on the understanding that his opponents would also desist. He would send a letter to the Pope excusing himself for having gone too far, and assuring him that his intention had not been to set himself against the Church of Rome. Further he would publish an appeal for obedience to Rome, recognizing that his words and writings had, perhaps, outstripped his thoughts.

To these three points, Spalatin and von Feilitzsch added a fourth: that the case should be entrusted to Cardinal Lang, Archbishop of Salzburg, who was surrounded by learned and impartial men. Luther said he was ready to accept the cardinal's judgement, as far as he was able; otherwise, he would maintain his appeal to the Council. In short, Luther conceded all that was wanted, so long as he was not asked to retract.

The next day he again appeared before Miltitz with a draft of his letter to the Pope. It didn't take the commissioner long to realise that it would be useless to send it to Rome. Luther regretted that his duty to the Church obliged him to do what he was being reproached for; he said that he did not know what to do in order to cease incurring the Pope's anger. If it was enough to retract his theses in order to bring peace to the Church, he would do so immediately. But his ideas were now no longer his own. They had been adopted by so many educated Germans that he would do great harm to the Roman Church in retracting them. His accusers were the ones who should be incriminated. It was they who brought the Church into disrepute by hiding behind the Pope to satisfy their greed. The Holy Father could be assured that Luther had never wished to blame the Pope's authority nor that of the Roman Church. He accepted without qualification the supreme power of the Church which was second only to that of Christ. In all, Luther desired only one thing: that money should cease corrupting the Church, that the people should no longer be led into error, that they should be taught to prefer charity to indulgences. The rest did not matter.

Careful not to jeopardise his position by being too intransigent, Miltitz contented himself with Luther's double undertaking neither to write on indulgences nor to publish corrections. On his side, he promised to ask the Pope to appoint a learned bishop to draw up the list of theses to be retracted.

With the agreement concluded, Miltitz took everyone to dine at the castle. The wine loosened his tongue. He declared that he had established on the way that of every five persons, three were for Luther and only two for Rome. No matter had embarrassed the Curia so much for the last ten years. It would prefer to lose ten million ducats rather than see this case drawn out any further.

Luther was not fooled by these extravagant statements. He could have asked how the Curia would make up the loss of these ducats. But he let himself be harangued and even embraced by the commissioner whom wine made affectionate as well as garrulous.

Miltitz was very pleased with these two days during which he had at times been moved to tears. Before leaving, he called on the Elector, who made him agree to his friend Richard of Greiffenklau, Archbishop Elector of Trier, as Luther's judge: Cardinal Lang definitely had too bad a character!

Then he stopped at Leipzig to deal with Tetzel. He still thought that here was the man to sort out first. In any case, it would be good to make an example. The Dominican superior brought him a poor, sick, demoralised man. The proud preacher whose followers used to flock round him was only a shadow of himself. Luther's knock-out blow had felled him. In disgrace in Mainz and at Rome, he had to endure the scrutiny of his accounts by the apostolic commissioner, assisted by a Fugger accountant. It appeared that he had helped himself – no more than any other, in fact not too badly – to money, horses, servants. One of the evils of the indulgence system was that half the proceeds (at least of the money) never reached its destination; the rake-off began at the source, with the preacher himself.

Miltitz declared, severely, that he would make his report to Rome and that more would be heard of it. But Tetzel never recovered.

It remained to draft the other report dealing with Luther. In his best hand, Miltitz wrote to Leo X that, despite all Luther's faults, he had no intention of blaming the Pope, the Apostolic See or the Roman Church. It was Tetzel who was the cause of his errors. Luther had only tried to suppress the Dominican's abuses, and it was true he went too far. But after reflection, he was touched with a sincere and profound regret for his excesses of language. He was ready to revoke everything even in writing, publicly to proclaim his error and promise not to continue with it. He would already have revoked everything in the Legate's presence if the latter had not taken Tetzel's side and been too hard with Luther.

Now nothing remained but for the happy commissioner to seek out his patron, the Cardinal-Legate, on whom he had just played such a nasty trick.

12

Stalemate

Emperor Maximilian had expected to be in Augsburg for Epiphany, 1519. But it happened that his constitution could not endure the gastronomic excesses of that season of the year, and on 12 January he died. The news travelled along the snow-covered roads of Europe, and the Christian world awoke, one fine morning, on the threshold of a new era.

Frederick of Saxony was the first to be informed. When there was a vacancy on the throne, responsibility for the Empire reverted to him. He was in supreme authority in Germany until the election of the new emperor, and indeed until his corona-tion. His first task was to see to this election. It would take place in June, at Frankfurt-on-the-Main.

The courier arrived in Rome on 23 January and the Pope officially informed the cardinals on the following day. But by then a messenger was already on his way to Germany, carrying detailed instructions – and money – to the Legate Cajetan.

'In the general interest, as much as in the interest of the Holy See, the Pope prefers that a German prince be elected. You should see whether the Elector of Saxony is not in the best position to obtain a majority but, in any event, under no circumstances should it be the King of Spain.' Three months earlier, the Legate had been threatening Frederick the Wise with the Roman anathema, but now the demands of papal politics obliged him to revise his attitude completely.

The report made to him by Charles Miltitz, which arrived while this was going on, aroused no reaction on his part. He had dealt with the Luther case and he had less time than ever to give it any thought. If the private chamberlain had obtained a successful result where he had failed, so much the better. He hoped that Luther's good disposition, for which Miltitz vouched, would not turn out to be a delusion.

January was not over before the Curia had changed its horse. Charles of Spain had going for him the treaty signed in August by Maximilian with four of the seven electors. He was too powerful for the Elector of Saxony to take on. Besides, Charles had at his disposal the colossal fortune of the Fuggers, and they had an interest in favouring the sovereign who controlled the minerals of Styria and the port of Antwerp, the pillars of their financial empire. It was necessary, therefore, to change to the other candidate in the race, whom the papacy at first wanted to ignore: the King of France.

It was by no means certain that the Germans would accept a French emperor. But Francis I's electoral campaign would cut down the chances of his rival and might open the way at the last moment for the Elector of Saxony to succeed. One of the additional benefits of this plan was that the two kings would be so embroiled with each other that they would be unable to act in concert against the Holy See for some time to come.

At the beginning of March, Archbishop Robert Orsini was also sent to Germany, armed with letters of introduction to each of the electors. He was to promote the King of France's candidature with all the means at his disposal. On the 12th, the latter was authorized to promise cardinals' hats to the Electors of Trier and Cologne. Albert of Mainz, already invested with the purple, was to be offered the coveted role of permanent legate in Germany. Everyone capable of tipping the balance in favour of Francis I was besieged by papal agents, and badgered by letters from the Curia.

As everyone expected, the electors took no notice of the agreement concluded with the dead emperor. Each one had much to gain by leaving his final vote uncertain to the last moment. Most of the electors pocketed the money of the last bidder without turning a hair, while the opponent's agents were waiting in the antechamber. In this style of operating the honours went to Joachim of Brandenburg.

Frederick the Wise showed himself to be as incorruptible as he had been in August, at Augsburg. Despite certain irritating debts he declined the advances of the royal candidates. Only the Curia could hope to influence him, thanks to the Luther case which was in a fair way to becoming 'providential' for Rome.

Miltitz had sent very reassuring news. He had kept his promise to Luther to do everything to reach an accommodation with the Pope. Leo X was pleased to have regained control over one of those dangerous men about whom vigilance was essential.

Since the imperial Vicar, Frederick the Wise, was so taken with his professor, had not the moment come to use one to work on the other? The idea was so attractive that, solely on the basis of the information supplied by Miltitz, it was decided to send to the 'notorious heretic' a letter from his Holiness himself.

The text, penned by the humanist Sadoleto, was addressed 'to my dear son Martin Luther, of the Eremite order of St Augustine, professor of theology'. The Pope declared himself happy to have received good news at last. Considering that the spirit is willing but the flesh weak, and that many things said under the sway of anger are put right later after reflection, he gave thanks to God for having deigned to enlighten the heart of Doctor Martin and having seen to it that the faithful, who submitted to his authority and to whom he dispensed his teaching could no longer be misled into errors so serious and so pernicious on questions which touched the salvation of souls. As Vicar of the One who did not desire the death of a sinner but rather that he should turn from his sin and live, the Pope accepted Luther's apologies with a paternal heart. And by virtue of the goodwill which he accorded to all learned men who applied themselves to literature, and especially to the Holy Scripture, he wanted to see and hear Luther in private. In this way, Brother Martin could freely and in complete safety make before the Vicar of Christ the retraction which he feared to do before the Legate. As soon as he received this letter, he should set out and come directly to meet the Pope, without ill-will or anger in his heart, but with a peaceful disposition, full of the Holy Spirit and of love. The sovereign pontiff was assured that, in such a frame of mind, Luther would do all that the praise of almighty God demanded, and that he would have the joy of knowing what an affectionate and lenient father he had in Leo X. . . .

The message was sent, as was proper, to the Elector of Saxony, through diplomatic channels. It was up to the prince to decide what was to be done with it.

The imperial Vicar could reflect with satisfaction that a time had not been fixed to the summons. Its terms, which were firm and definite but not harsh, showed well enough that the Pope was making a gesture to Luther. There was certainly no reason to suspect a trap. The amazing leniency shown twice before by Leo X towards the traitorous cardinals was reason enough to believe in his sincerity. It was equally clear that the natural consequence of the interview would be Luther's elevation to some important position. Leo X, who understood men, honoured his opponents in equal measure to the price he put on their submission.

The only shadow across the picture was that it was based on the inconsistent reports of Miltitz. Luther had never said that he was ready to retract, and the Elector knew very well that he had not changed his mind. He had just received from him an eloquent letter in which the monk had assured him that he only had to say the word and he, Luther, would disappear. It was from the prince that Luther held his university chair, which made it his duty to speak out, but his Highness could withdraw his trust in him. The dilemma was confined for the moment to the alternatives: whether to dismiss Luther from his office, or maintain the *status quo*. The Elector did not find it disagreeable to be in the end the only man in the world able to silence the stubborn fellow. That was a trump card which was by no means negligible vis à vis Rome, and a trump card was not given for nothing.

Miltitz had at least obtained Luther's silence, and on this

point, Luther kept his promise. He had published the promised explanations, in the manner required by Miltitz, that is to say, by trying to calm the spirits and dispose them better towards Rome. A new written communication from Prierias had elicited no reaction from him.

The prince, who was accurately kept abreast of things by Spalatin, knew that the monk would have nothing to do with the Pope's invitation. It was not for him to expound, but for those who found errors in his writings. He wasn't asking for a father, but for a Pope who stood for the Gospel. The pontiff who ruled in Rome seemed to him to be a caricature of a pope, a plaything of the Antichrist who was using him in his bid to seize the Church. Luther was sincere when he said that he would submit to the authority of Rome; but he spoke in the same way about the Sultan's authority. For him, all authority was a matter of providence, and the Pope's was no exception. In his eyes, it was purely human, an historical reality, no more. He expected from it only the freedom to consider in peace the mystery which he alone seemed to have discovered, and which he had failed to persuade the Church hierarchy to acknowledge. He wasn't going to lift a finger to give satisfaction to the Pope. He had nothing more to say to him.

The imperial Vicar could pass on the papal letter without comment, as he had done on so many similar occasions. However, he was anxious to avoid a new scandal which would give ammunition to the Curia. And, if Luther were persuaded to go to Rome, he would probably he kept there for a time at least as a hostage. The Elector would be put under a pressure which was at odds with his independence. The obvious solution was to file the letter away; Luther was never to receive it.

Frederick was not the only one to find Rome's meddling in the affairs of the Empire rather heavy-handed. The ecclesiastical electors, that is to say, the three Archbishops of Mainz, Trier and Cologne, resented the directives presumptuously given them. Charles of Spain, moreover, pointed out that demonstrations of popular support for him in Germany and the

Swiss cantons made it clear that there was no question of the crown passing to a French prince.

Leo X appeared to lose his composure a little, and sent Cajetan, on 4 May, a letter which gave him the power to declare Francis I elected, even if he obtained only three votes. It must be said, in the Pope's defence, that he had just been cruelly stricken by the deaths within the space of a few weeks, of his nephew Lorenzo's wife in childbirth, and of Lorenzo himself, of syphilis. The child of the two ill-fated people was a little girl, Catherine de Medici. Leo X resolved at least not to show so much favouritism to the 'Florentines', his kinsmen whom Luther reproached for having sponged off him.

On 29 May Rome acknowledged that Francis I had lost any hope of being elected. Advances were made, on the off chance, to the King of England, Henry VIII, and an English diplomat was at Frankfurt. But the time had come for the Curia to play its last card: Frederick the Wise.

On 7 June the papal representatives and the French ambassador received an instruction, drafted in great haste, that they insist that Frederick vote for the King of France, or, if possible, that he manoeuvre to obtain the crown for himself. If he could obtain two votes in addition to his own, the Pope would recognize the election and would declare it alone to be valid.

This overture ended in total failure. The imperial Vicar politely showed his visitors out, and the Germans took umbrage: three days later, at Mainz, the nuncio Orsini had to escape in disguise. The other nuncio, Caracciolo, who was ill, had himself carried in a litter to the Archbishop of Mainz to invite him to 'consider the well-being of the Church', but it was all in vain. The Elector of Trier, who looked after the interests of the French king, let the Pope know that Charles of Spain was assured of four votes. It had become useless and dangerous to oppose him. The election was to be held on the 28th.

Considering that it was useless, as he wrote to Cajetan, to beat his head against a wall, Leo X decided on 17 June to sign a treaty with the Spanish ambassador, removing the major obstacle put forward by the papacy for some months: the forbidden union of the crowns of Naples and Rome. The Holy See accepted that union – but only in this particular instance. The Spaniards considered the possibility of dispensing altogether with the papal authorization, but it was more advantageous to allow the Pope to save face. For the news of the treaty, soon sent to Frankfurt, made it known to all that from now on the Pope set no store in anyone except the King of Spain.

But before the couriers had arrived at their destination, the papal agents at Frankfurt had again tried to win over the Saxon Elector to the papal policy. To do this, they availed themselves of the services of Charles Miltitz, who had been very restless for some months, not having done anything special but who was still assumed to be in charge of the Luther case. The same question was put again very cleverly: 'Vote for Francis I, that is, for yourself.' As part of the deal a cardinal's hat was offered for one of the prince's subjects. Peutinger had already spoken of this the previous winter. The hat which Luther scorned to go and seek in Rome would be placed on his head by order of the higher authorities.

But Frederick had neither the ability nor the necessary power to manage all 400 German states. As his nickname indicated, he was 'Wise'. He firmly declined the offer, which moreover had lapsed before it had even been made. Francis I, likewise, withdrew at the last minute from the competition. He was no more anxious than Rome or Frederick to be the loser.

There were to be no losers. Charles of Spain, the only candidate, was unanimously elected King of the Romans by the seven votes of the electoral college, on 28 June. It cost him a small fortune, a cool million ducats: Francis I's bill was a little less, but he had already lost everything but his honour.

Leo X, while sending the customary congratulations, continued to think of Frederick: 'If the King of France had followed our advice, a third candidate would have been elected.' As a scapegoat was needed, all the blame fell again on Cajetan who disappeared from the scene.

For the moment, Frederick the Wise retained his prerogative as imperial Vicar. The new Emperor was still in Spain. He would not be expected in Germany for some months. His agents relieved the Elector of the worry of his obligations and Miltitz was at last getting ready to deliver to him the famous Rose. The pleasure moreover would be solely the apostolic commissioner's: the prince would send some of his people to fetch the papal distinction, and would see that the bearer be given 200 florins as a tip.

13
The Leipzig Dispute

While Frankfurt made merry in celebration of the election of a stranger, the city of Leipzig was in a state of excitement. In the streets and the public squares, there was talk only of the disputation which was going to pit Doctor Luther against the formidable Doctor Eck, the vice-chancellor of the University of Ingolstadt.

The event had attracted a considerable crowd of masters and students, of learned men and monks of all orders. The innkeepers rubbed their hands with glee, despite the daily scuffles between the partisans of the two champions. It was arranged that Duke George of Saxony's castle would be the venue of the debate as the University did not have a large enough room. The choir-school of the Church of St Thomas performed a Mass in twelve voices!

Doctor Eck was to be seen among the ranks of the faculty of theology, during the Corpus Christi procession. And it was then that the arrival of the party from Wittenberg was announced.

Surrounded by two hundred students armed with pikes and halberds, two carts slowly made their way through the crowd. In the first, Doctor Karlstadt, a small unprepossessing man. Behind him, Doctor Luther himself, chatting intimately with his friend Melanchthon and the Duke of Pomerania. In theory, Karlstadt was Eck's principal opponent. But everyone knew that the real confrontation would take place with Luther.

With a jolt, an axle on the first vehicle broke, and the unfortunate Karlstadt was thrown to the ground under an avalanche of massive volumes which he had stacked around

93

him. While he was given help to marshal his 'ammunition'
Luther went on to refresh himself at his printer's house.

He learned that the Bishop had forbidden the disputation.
But the Duke had the notices seized and the man distributing
them thrown into prison: he was determined that the meeting
should take place, and he made John Eck welcome.

Luther did not expect the same treatment. Karlstadt was the
one officially invited by the Duke. The University itself had for
some time refused to authorize the 'heretic's' visit. Founded a
century before by the professors and students of the prestigeous
University of Prague, who were hostile to Hussitism, Leipzig
University had a tradition of stern orthodoxy. The Duke
insisted that John Eck, who had undertaken to provide the
definitive refutation of Luther, be given the opportunity to do
the Church such a conspicuous service.

The agreement with Miltitz prevented Luther from resuming
the controversy. The dispute between Karlstadt and Eck, in
which Luther himself had taken the initiative at Augsburg, did
not now concern him. Why was it necessary for Eck to take him
to task on the theses which he had published at the end of
December, ostensibly to set down clearly for Karlstadt the
subject of the discussion? Eck not only intervened in the debate
on indulgences, he gave exaggerated importance to a passing
remark made by Luther in his *Explanations*, that the Roman
Church had had no supremacy over the Eastern Church before
the time of St Gregory the Great (590–604). Luther had in
mind the historical situation, which had for long been fluid,
and the late development of a *legal* concept of papal primacy.
Except from a strictly dogmatic view, the phrase 'the Roman
Church for some centuries was not *above* other Churches'
scarcely deserved to be re-examined. But Eck was a theologian
and he had twisted Luther's statement to make him say that the
Roman Church had not been superior to the other Churches
during the first centuries. That distortion, perhaps, had not
been intentional, for the papalism of the time often played
around with shades of meaning without even realizing what

they were. Eck, however, was itching to have it out with Luther, and had done everything to push him into an extreme position.

Provoked, Luther could do nothing but reply. This had been the opinion of the University of Wittenberg and the Elector found no objections. Luther, therefore, accepted the challenge and drew up thirteen theses in reply to those of Eck.

It was said that his case would never be decided. 'God no longer leads me, he drags me along, and pushes me ahead. I am no longer master, to do what I wish. I long for rest, and I must be thrown into agitation and tumult.' Even before the disputation, expected at the end of June, the truce had been broken by the Franciscans of Jüterbog, who had denounced Luther as a heretic to the Bishop of Brandenburg.

In the morning of 27 June, the solemn mass for the opening of the disputation took place. Then, in the great hall of the Castle of Pleissenburg, an academic meeting assembled, during which the learned Father Mosellan held forth for two hours, in a discourse of interminably long and inaudible sentences. Seventy-five citizens armed with pikes mounted guard at all the strategic places, but this was not the day that they would have to intervene. Everyone waited stoically until Mosellan had finished his dissertation on 'the art of disputation in theological matters'.

The next day, Karlstadt opened fire. Eck was a giant, gifted with a powerful and resonant voice. He seemed more like a butcher or a soldier than a theologian. But for a long time he had been past master in the art of disputation, so dear to Mosellan. His wily spirit was served by a prodigious memory. He boasted of having known the Bible by heart from the age of twelve. . . . But did he understand it? His pleasure when he succeeded in squeezing his opponent in his dialectical grip made him sometimes forget the object of the discussion.

Following the practice of German universities, the two champions could speak in turn, and each had to speak slowly enough for the copyists to take notes as the debate proceeded. Eck had tried to impose the 'Italian' method, in which the best man won at each point, with each one speaking when he wanted to, and even at the same time as the other. It had been necessary to settle before a notary on this by no means negligible detail, and others. It was decided moreover that the victor in the contest should be named by the Universities of Erfurt and Paris, to which the written proceedings of the debate would be sent.

The first question chosen was that of free will, that is to say, of man's part in preparing the way for grace. Catholic dogma was that the sinner always retained a certain freedom to do good. But for the Wittenbergers, the human will was only free when it had been freed by grace. Karlstadt rummaged in his notes and dictated his phrases word by word to the copyists. Eck was exasperated, and he was not the only one. The accident suffered on entering the town was more than a bad omen: it had deprived the Wittenberg representative of some of his aids. Besides, the discussion didn't interest him. It was with Luther that he wanted to cross swords, and for whom he had come. It was time to pass on to serious matters.

The confrontation took place at first in the form of preaching. 29 and 30 June and 2 July were holidays, and each of them put forward his views in a sermon to a full house.

While waiting for Karlstadt to finish – he took until 3 July – Luther had some spare time, and used it to walk about the town. Coming one day upon the Dominican monastery, he went into the church. Immediately, like a flight of sparrows, priests in chasubles shot out of all the chapels, interrupting their masses to go and cover the sacred Host and the chalice, and hastily gathered in the Holy Sacrament.

Luther was riveted to the spot. He was the devil in person, or worse still, the heretic. He was not worthy of communion, and they wouldn't even allow him to see the consecrated bread and wine.

In one of the monastery cells, Tetzel was dying, unknown to Luther. When he learned of it, he sent a word of consolation.

'Do not reproach yourself. This affair was begun by one other than yourself.'

On 4 July, at 7 in the morning, the moment at last arrived for which John Eck had been waiting so eagerly. Opposite him, in the chair decorated by a statue of St Martin, sat an ascetic-looking man whose bones one could almost count. His calm smile disturbed the man who had overwhelmed Karlstadt easily. Perhaps Luther could not shout louder than he could, but his voice was clear and easily heard. Generally he showed a disarming simplicity, taking things and people as they came. But when he was aroused, phrases of faultless logic crowded on his lips like close-ranked battalions, and it was then that John Eck was conscious of his own weakness: he was brilliant, but not profound. The *Asterisks* which Luther had addressed to him the year before, in reply to his *Obelisks* about the theses on indulgences, guaranteed that the game was far from being won.

For, the Eck of the *Obelisks* had to defeat the Luther of the *Asterisks*. At Augsburg, the Wittenberg monk had kept the authority of the Church at bay by asking for a disputation which Cajetan had been in no position to grant. As long as it stopped at that point, Luther could bluff and win every time. But today, this disputation was taking place and he, John Eck, was the one who had set it afoot. He had worked for some months, he had stepped up the proceedings, including those concerning Luther himself. And he had hooked his fish by the theses written at the end of December. Luther's reply went much further than his previous writings. This time, the violation against papal power was flagrant. All he had to do was to make the audience aware of this and be his witness. The room was packed to the rafters: the faculty of theology was there in full strength, with its dean, Dungersheim; there were also monastery abbots, monks, Duke George's chaplain, Jerome Emser, but . . . not a single Dominican!

Luther studied the St George under whose aegis his colleague's fight with the new dragon was being held, with an air of detachment. He had observed Eck's trickery in the debate with Karlstadt, and knew that his opponent was tough and dangerous. He sensed also that Eck would not allow himself, any more than Cajetan or Miltitz, to be drawn into a serious analysis of Scriptural revelation.

However, that was the heart of the debate. The papal decretals based Roman primacy on Scripture. But the biblical message was above all the declaration of faith in Christ. The Church was only to be found where the Word of God was preached and received in faith. The Church was above all the home of believers, and its lord was invisible, for he was none other than Christ, the object of faith. By contrast, the theologians and jurists drew from the Scripture, by distorting it, the idea that the Church had a visible head, the Pope, and that it was an earthly empire. But faith could recognize no other lord than Christ. The Pope was at most a sovereign by human right, and this right, unknown for hundreds of years, had come to light only in recent centuries. The Eastern Church had never in practice been under the jurisdiction of Rome, and this had not prevented it from being a true Christian Church. In short, the dogma of papal primacy flew in the face of biblical and historical truth.

These conclusions had only come to Luther's mind in the months he had spent studying the question of primacy for the disputation. At first he had been amazed: papal authority had never appeared to him before in that light. He was surprised to have found its evidence so flimsy. Doubting what he should do as a result of such discoveries, he would willingly resign himself to silence. But Eck had already exposed him publicly, and it was too late to draw back. He was the first to speak.

'Out of respect for the Pope and the Roman Church,' he began, 'I would have preferred to put to one side this question of the primacy. It is Dr Eck who has obliged me to speak of it. But before beginning on this subject, I must express my astonishment at not seeing in this room any of those who, in recent times, have so often called me a heretic, in public or in private. . . .'

Everyone understood this allusion to the Dominicans. Their absence at least allowed the meeting to proceed without incident. Passions were not yet aroused and Luther could calmly explain his observations and his doubts.

However, the contest was not going to take place on the subject of Roman primacy, but on the question of the infallibility of Councils. The next day, Eck couldn't resist the desire to pose a 'stinger': the way in which Luther explained primacy was reminiscent of the Hussites who rejected papal authority. Luther shrugged his shoulders, but Eck insisted: 'If the reverend Father is really against the Hussites, why doesn't he put his talents to work by writing against them?'

Thus did the master of disputation lay his trap! Luther had seen others since the time he had taken part in university contests. He quickly retorted,

'Among the articles of John Hus and the Hussites are many which are truly Christian and the Church could not condemn them, for example the phrase "There is only *one* universal Church".'

Luther failed to obtain the desired effect. Leipzig was the last place to speak well of the Hussites! Duke George, who was present at the gathering that day, threw up his arms,

'That's the plague!'

Eck triumphantly recorded this first demonstration of heresy in the indulgences man. The phrase quoted by Luther had been explicitly condemned because Hus meant 'Church Universal' in the exclusive sense of a 'Church of the predestined', whereas the Church was a community of righteous men and sinners. Luther lifted it out of context. No matter, in a disputation anything goes. Eck would now try to push Luther to give himself away more and more.

'You don't shrink, then, from accusing of error a Council as holy and ecumenical as that of Constance, which condemned the article in question?'

'I have never thought of saying anything at all against the Council of Constance.'

It was true. Luther had only sent up a trial balloon to see how the other would react. It was a fair enough tactic, and Eck countered by turning it against him: to defend a thesis condemned by a council was, logically, to accuse the council of error. But Luther did not intend to make a dogmatic declaration on the infallibility of councils. Doctor Eck sensed that his opponent was beginning to get out of his depth. He declared that he would undertake to prove from Luther's words and writings that he had indeed spoken against the Council of Constance. Now the Germans had a special affection for that council, it was *their* council: the Emperor Sigismund had put an end there to the papal schism, and sent John Hus to the stake, even though he had given him safe conduct. The fact that there was still a Roman papacy was due to the Germans, and not for the first time. To speak against Constance was not only sacrilege but a crime of treason.

'You are the Hussites' patron!'

'Still babbling on!' said Luther.

Contrary to the agreement made before the disputation, Eck was setting himself up as judge. The contest was degenerating into a trial.

'I have not approved of the errors of Hus,' Luther made clear. 'I would like Doctor Eck to prove to me that the articles which I have described as Christian are erroneous.'

Again the same mysterious demand. Luther was searching among his judges for one who would speak of the Bible as he, Luther, had learned to do.

Eck beat a retreat; personal attacks were, in fact, forbidden: 'I did not say that the reverend Father was a heretic, but declared that his assertions were favourable to the views of heretics, particularly the Hussites.'

The tension reached its highest point. They returned to the question of papal primacy. Eck had no difficulty in countering Luther's thesis. All he needed to do was to draw on the rich papalist literature of the times. But he lacked as much as Luther did a good theology of the Church. His thesis, which was that of the Roman tradition, was worth more than his arguments. Doubtless it would have been better, in view of the climate of ideas at that time, to forego launching a debate for which neither of the two participants was properly prepared. An exclamation of Duke George, which Luther recalled, was perfect evidence of the vague idea which faithful Catholics then had of papal primacy: 'Whether the Pope has his authority by divine right, or human right, he is Pope.' If one had to talk of heresy, it was no greater on one side than the other.

But for everyone, there was only one heretic in the room. The hounds scented blood and Luther was not going to escape them. At one point, he made the mistake of declaring:

'Doctor Eck must prove first that the councils cannot be wrong and are never wrong . . .'

Eck, who had to wait his turn to take up the debate, had time to prepare his reply. He finally declared, solemnly:

'Reverend Father! If you believe that a council legitimately assembled has been in error or could be in error, you are no longer to me anything but a heathen and a publican. I forbear pronouncing the word "heretic". '

But Luther had had enough:

'Conciliar declarations are not words of God for me. I do not consider myself bound in conscience by them.'

'The judges of the disputation will decide.'

It was over. The Vice-Chancellor had got what he wanted, he had led the Wittenberger to profess heresy publicly. The last days of the meeting consisted of discussions on purgatory, indulgences and penitence. Karlstadt, who had recovered his composure and rediscovered his thread of ideas, took over from Luther, and defended skilfully enough the idea that the human will without grace can only sin.

But the Duke needed his premises. The Elector of Brandenburg was arriving from Frankfurt with all his retinue: away with disputing and disputations!

While awaiting the verdict of the universities chosen as judges, each man checked his balance sheet. Karlstadt had acquired a young deer, a gift from Duke George. Luther had received nothing, as the Duke pretended to ignore him. But many at Leipzig were won over: students, and even professors, migrated *en masse* to Wittenberg.

Eck was taken to be the victor. He granted himself a soldier's leave, although his allusions 'to the fine beer of Leipzig and the beautiful worshippers of Venus' should not lead one to imagine the worst. For him, the Duke's consideration was worth a deer, payment of his expenses and a reception at the court. The Bishop of Brandenburg asked his advice on the denunciation of Luther by the Franciscans of Jüterbog. In two hours, he gained another fifteen victor's wreaths!

Making the most of his advantage, Eck got a horse and went looking for Prince Frederick to persuade him to abandon a cause which was now lost. But the Prince was content to send him back to Luther and Karlstadt. Eck wasn't to be put off so easily for so little and denounced Luther to the Dominican Hoogstraten, Germany's grand inquisitor and the thorn in Reuchlin's side. Then he tore up the account of the disputation which that beardless youth Melanchthon had been allowed to publish. On his return to Ingolstadt, he would find out what victory was really like.

But it was on the Roman side especially that Eck tried his luck. He had sent off a detailed report of the dispute and on Luther's heresy. Thanks to him, a major obstacle had been removed. Rome could not but be grateful to him for having taken away from Luther the excuse that nobody would agree to debate with him.

The humanists, among whom Eck was proud to number himself, did not forgive him. At Wittenberg, Nuremberg, Augsburg, Strasbourg, Selestat, Heidelberg, Erfurt and even Leipzig, pamphlets against Eck rained down. Erasmus declared that Luther was too honest and would pay for it, but that 'J. Eck was only a *jeck*, a fool'. Lazarus Spengler of Nuremberg and Bernard Adelmann of Augsburg stood out in this campaign. The finishing stroke was given by Willibald Pirckheimer, who

made the whole of Germany laugh by offering his account of
'the debagging of Eck'.

14
The Universities' Verdict

The masters of the University of Paris were not in the least surprised at the appeal addressed to them from Leipzig by Duke George of Saxony. For some centuries, the prestige of Paris stood high throughout Christendom. Duke George never imagined for a moment that he was doing the illustrious doctors of Paris a favour by consulting them, and he was right: it was he, rather, who was honoured in soliciting their advice.

But the authority of the judges he had chosen was matched only by their prudence. There was no question of their recklessly launching themselves into a matter in which the Holy See was involved. To gain time, they began by asking for twenty-four printed copies of the proceedings of the dispute. Each of the members of the jury had to have every facility for examining them at leisure. And, as time was precious, his Lordship would do well to send a little money . . . seven hundred golden crowns! In spite of his zeal for good causes, Duke George felt the bill was a bit high for his purse and no more was said about it.

For its part, the University of Erfurt, Luther's *alma mater*, was greatly embarrassed. It had to decide between one of its most brilliant students and a doctor for whom no one had any time. It had to be wary of the Archbishop of Mainz, on whom it was legally dependent, and at the same time cope with public opinion which was stirred up and entirely under the influence of the humanists, who were on Luther's side. After some months of vacillation, the university opted out of the matter on 9 December. The mission entrusted to it was too formidable to handle. In the end the anticipated judgement came from two universities who had not been asked at all! Cologne and Louvain.

At the end of 1518 a volume printed in Basle and containing various writings of the two Wittenberg prima donnas, Luther and Karlstadt, was circulating in Louvain. It included Luther's theses on indulgences, his *Explanations*, the reply to Prierias' *Dialogue*, the sermons on indulgences and on excommunication, and two other sermons on penitence and preparation for the reception of the Eucharist.

The theology faculty, concerned in this case as in others about doctrinal orthodoxy, had got hold of the work and submitted it to a painstaking examination. Luther was already so widely regarded as a suspect character that there was no need to study his doctrine on its merits. That doctrine appeared to contain heretical ideas, and it had to be considered from that point of view. A theology faculty showed its competence more clearly by its flair for unmasking heresy than by contributing to the progress of Christian thought, which could easily become risky. The Church had always had a horror of innovators. Before thinking of improving on official teaching, which was for the most part good enough for the people, it was necessary to preserve the integrity of the apostolic tradition.

When the masters of Louvain came together to pronounce on the writings of the man from Wittenberg, the sole item on the agenda was a list of the errors which were known to be found therein. It was a serious matter both for the accused theologian and his judges. And, as there was no hurry, it seemed prudent to ask the advice of their colleagues in Cologne, before concluding the matter.

So it was that on 30 August 1519 the theology faculty at Cologne denounced a selection of Martin Luther's theses, taken from the same Basle edition, and recommended that he be banned and his works burned, while at the same time requiring him to make a public retraction.

Cologne was no more interested than Louvain in the basis of the problem, but was content to reproach Luther for teaching that good works cannot be carried out without sin because the will of the sinner is not free, for distorting the Bible and the sayings of the Church Fathers, for falsifying their meaning, for denigrating the sacrament of penance against the teaching and practice of the universal Church, for asserting that God remits simultaneously the guilt and the reparation which it requires, for denying without good reason the existence of a treasury of indulgences, and thereby wronging the saints, for teaching absurdities on purgatory, for adopting heresies already condemned on the primacy of the Roman Church and its privilege of being superior to all the Churches, for scoffing at the apostolic see; and reducing the power of the Pope by asserting that the sovereign pontiff could remit only the penalties which he himself had imposed.

Reassured by such an unequivocal stance, the faculty of Louvain also publicly pronounced its judgement on 7 November. In addition to the ideas censured by Cologne, it brought forward yet another series of errors: Luther despised philosophy and the doctors of the last four centuries; he asserted that the grace of God was the only source in man of the desire for forgiveness; that without this preliminary grace man could only approach the sacraments with selfish motives; he placed faith so much above contrition that he saw a heresy in the idea that contrition is a condition for the remission of sins; he departed from the teaching of the Church on the examination of conscience, venial sin and mortal sin; he blamed the Church for not having taken sins of omission seriously; he said that God required man to do the impossible, with the result that everyone sinned continually; he accused all the children of Adam of being idolators; salvation, according to him, was not fulfilling the law, which he declared to be impossible, but the recognition that we can only transgress it; moral virtues and also theological speculation were impious and deceitful as long as the heart had not been purified by the grace of God.

And thus, in the wake of John Eck, the great Catholic universities came to the aid of the papacy to define in a precise fashion the heresy intuitively sensed from the beginning. Luther could no longer say that they refused to point out his errors.

But in their eagerness to render the Church a service which she had not asked of them, the doctors of Cologne and Louvain had greatly simplified the controversy. Luther expected nothing of those whose only thought was to renew Prierias' gambit. Anyone could find something to criticize, even in the shortest of an author's writing. That wasn't the point.

While his case was in this way being attended to, Luther had resumed his usual activities at Wittenberg. He had returned from Leipzig without acknowledging defeat but nevertheless rather discouraged. Eck had called the tune from beginning to end, and the calm discussion on the doctrine of the Bible which he was desperately looking for had not taken place. In that capital of anti-Hussitism, he had not been able to prevent his opponent from sticking on him the infamous label of 'Hussite' and 'Bohemian'. When so compared with the most recent major heresy, his doctrine would inevitably attract every polemical attack, and he must expect to see renewed activity from the Roman judges who had been so difficult to get rid of.

In an attempt to avert the danger, he published in August, in quick succession, an exposition of his thesis on papal power, the *Explanations* of the thirteen theses of Leipzig, along with a detailed account of the dispute, and a biting reply to Eck's insolent intervention in his controversy with the Jüterbog Franciscans. But he had to admit that Eck had managed to give a decisive impetus to the campaign aimed at destroying him. Every day new difficulties loomed, and he was driven onto the defensive.

Without knowing whether he could ever regain the advantage, he at least tried to follow through the implications of the ideas for which he had given up his peace and quiet. The printers could no longer cope, and he had to employ up to three at a time. Every week, scores of manuscript pages went to the typesetter. In September, his commentary on the Epistle to the

Galatians was printed and began to be circulated. The Elector had returned ill from Frankfurt, and Luther drew to his attention a little spiritual writing in which he counselled him to rely, in his ordeal, on the passion of Christ and the goodness of God rather than the 'fourteen subsidiary saints'. Frederick was so impressed by it that he instructed Luther to prepare forthwith a series of sermons on the epistles and Gospels for the Sundays and feast days throughout the year. But, in addition to his courses and university work, Luther was already putting in a lot of work on a book on prayer, and another on the Lord's Prayer, not to mention his sermons on preparation for death, on penitence, baptism, the eucharist, excommunication (yet again!) and usury. (It was considered immoral at that time to extract interest for money lent, but the development of commercial exchanges was making this principle more and more oppressive and unworkable.) Leo X borrowed money at up to 40 per cent interest. Luther, who claimed no special revelation on this point, tried as so many others to run with the hare and hunt with the hounds.

Soon after Christmas he learned that the Bishop of Meissen had condemned his sermon on the eucharist. At the same time, Duke George had put pressure on Frederick to enforce sanctions against the author of the heretical remarks denounced by the Bishop.

He was reproached for asking for the restoration of communion in both kinds. For some centuries, the Church had reserved the chalice to the priest, which was not in accordance with primitive practice. Christ had distributed to the Apostles both bread and wine.

The importance of the 'novelty' advocated by Luther was that the Hussites had made it their symbol. Bohemian Christians, despite Rome, had resumed the custom of communication with bread and the chalice. The edition of Luther's sermon was illustrated with an engraving showing two vessels, one with the host, the other with the chalice: the allusion to Hussite ideas seemed clear. The heresy implied was that Christ would not be wholly present in the element of the bread, as Catholic teaching would have it.

Luther, it was true, had contented himself with making the textual point: 'I would think it appropriate for the Church to re-establish in a general council, the Communion in both kinds, hitherto reserved for the priest.' In saying this, he was certainly thinking more of the controversy between Pope and Council than of the eucharistic theses of Jan Hus. No matter! He felt a certain satisfaction in seeing that he was no longer reproached for having wanted to take Scripture literally. His theses on free will, grace and the authority of the Church no longer seemed to stir up anyone at Meissen or Leipzig.

The rush to identify his teaching with the Hussite heresy led to letting loose unverified rumours about his origins. He had been born in Prague, and the ideas of Wyclif, Hus's precursor, had been inculcated in him from infancy. Some were persuaded that his father was the devil himself. An old Leipzig nun had once attended Luther's mother, and she had heard rumours that a youth, probably a demon in human form, had fertilized her before her husband Hans had had relations with her. 'I expect,' Luther commented, 'they will claim next that I have wife and children in Bohemia! However, the story of my origins is quite straightforward. I was born at Eisleben and baptised there in St Peter's Church. Of course, I do not remember it, but I believe what my parents and neighbours told me. My father and mother came from Eisenach, and almost all my relatives are still there. There is no place where I am better known. If these people had thought that my parents were Bohemians, they would not have been so mad as to become my uncles, nephews and cousins. The Counts of Mansfeld, who are as trustworthy as anyone in the Empire, know very well how things stood with me. Afterwards my life was spent at the university and the monastery at Erfurt, until I came to Wittenberg. In fourteen years, I spent one year at Magdeburg.' And he added for Spalatin's benefit:

'Let it go on. Let them lie, pretend, and think what they

please! I want nothing so much as to be relieved of my task of teaching. I do not believe one can do theology without offending the Pope and the bishops. There is nothing that the Scriptures condemn as much as the abuse of holy things and the prelates cannot bear anyone saying this.

'As for me, I have sacrificed everything for the Lord's name. May his will be done! Who asked him to make me a doctor? If it was his will, it is his business alone. And if he should change his mind he has only to destroy me. Far from frightening me, persecution fills the sails of my spirit in an unbelievable way. Perhaps that is why the Scriptures compare demons to the wind. I ask only one thing, that God will look kindly on me in everything that takes place between Him and me.

'As for the machinations of men, let us commit them to the Lord in prayer and faith. What can they do? Kill me? They would only revive me to kill me again! Declare me a heretic? But Christ himself was condemned with the wicked, the seducers and the accursed! The thought of his passion fills me with extraordinary fervour. For many men, and important men at that, my ordeal seems beyond compare, yet in fact it is nothing. The truth is that we have turned our backs on difficulties and anxieties, that is to say, on the Christian life.

'I have decided to fear absolutely nothing, to despise all threats. If I were not afraid of compromising our prince, I would abandon all discretion and myself challenge these angry and desperate men.'

For the moment, he had no need of this strength of purpose for the question of the sermon on the eucharist proved abortive. The two dukes preferred not to aggravate the situation and compromised with the Bishop of Meissen. But soon the texts of the condemnations of Cologne and Louvain reached Wittenberg. The latter came with a letter from Charles V's former teacher, Adrian of Utrecht, cardinal and Archbishop of Tortosa, in Spain. He ridiculed Luther. 'Not even a theological student would have committed such outlandish errors.'

Speaking of these 'errors', Luther had just given his sermon on Good Works, which defined once and for all his concept of faith: it was a perfect starting-point, and good works were only the fruit. He replied to the 'asses of Cologne and Louvain' that he cared for their opinion as much as for the ranting of a drunken woman.

On that day, 29 March 1520, the approval which reached him from all Germany and the cultured world encouraged him to think that those who opposed with him were only trying to distract attention from their own ignorance. Miltitz's observation was confirmed again and again: for every papal supporter there were three for Luther.

15
Germany to Luther's Aid

Outside the University of Wittenberg, which had supported Luther for some time, the first to rally to his doctrines had been the humanists.

The Reuchlin affair had been a kind of dress rehearsal. Two camps had been formed, the traditionalists on one side, the progressives on the other. The motives behind the division were primarily intellectual. Zealots for liberty and 'good letters' confronted the devotees of a finicky and unvarnished orthodoxy. The enemy had nothing but faults, and nothing could be learned from him.

With his exclusive attachment to the Bible, Luther could not be classed among the traditionalists. That was enough for him to be considered a hero in the eyes of some, a heretic in the eyes of others. From this basic qualifying principle each man made what he wanted. It was no more difficult to attribute heresies to him than to make him a disciple of Erasmus. Everyone seemed to be mistaken about him.

Everyone, that is, except Staupitz. As superior of the 'observant congregation' when Luther had become a monk, he had discerned his genius. He it was who had given Luther to the Church, who had taught him to make God's mercy the starting point of the spiritual life rather than an object to seek out. He had placed him in the saddle and, so to speak, thrown him into the arms of the Elector of Saxony, who must often have bewailed the awkward gift to his fine University of Wittenberg.

But Staupitz's character was not equal to his intuition. When he saw things breaking up, he vanished from Luther's life. The Augsburg episode, when he discreetly bolted after releasing

Luther from his vows, was symptomatic. In vain did Luther address distressed letters to him: 'What can I say to you about myself? You neglect me too much. I stretch out towards you like a deprived child towards its mother's breast. I beg you, don't give up glorifying God, even in me, sinner that I am. Life is a burden to me, death makes me fearful, faith I lack. Christ knows that I have not wanted my own talents, except to be able to serve him. Tonight I dreamed of you. You had just left me and I cried bitterly and lamented. But with one gesture of your hand, you told me to be calm, for you would return.'

One of the last words of the teacher he had cherished so much had been: 'Remember, brother Martin, that you began everything in the name of our Lord Jesus Christ.' Luther had never forgotten this message which seemed to him to come from heaven. He had made it his standard of conduct. What he had begun did not come from him. He would not yield an inch on it.

Deprived of the support of the one man in the world with whom he was able to discuss freely the thoughts which haunted him day and night, he had to take all his decisions alone, and became accustomed to doing so. One difficult question at this time was what attitude to adopt to his increasing success.

His books, like the theses on indulgences before them, had been distributed everywhere. At the Frankfurt book fair in 1518, a consignment of 600 volumes left for Paris and Spain. Luther was read at the Sorbonne, and it was a matter of regret there that those who taught Scripture did not have the same freedom of thought as he did. A bookseller in Padua was handling distribution in Italy, not so much to make money as to stimulate a renewal of piety. Luther's writings were noticed in Brabant and in England. Three hundred copies of his reply to Prierias had been printed in Basle. Next to Erasmus, Luther had become the godsend of the printers.

The public who bought his books consisted above all of intellectuals, teachers and humanists. Luther's correspondents included the most celebrated names of the age: Mutian, Pirckheimer, Reuchlin, Capito and even Erasmus, the master of the humanist stream of thought who then lived in Basle, one of the cultural capitals of the age. Erasmus had viewed with sympathy Luther's resistance to the attempts made to silence him. The Wittenberg monk's theology would not spoil the movement which he himself had launched; he intervened many times in his favour, in particular with the Archbishop of Mainz.

Some bishops were equally favourable to Luther: the Bishop of Würzburg wrote to the Elector of Saxony that he should not allow anyone to blame the pious doctor Luther, as the proceedings against him were absolutely unjust; and the Swiss Archbishop Schinner declared: 'Eck can say what he wants, but it is Luther who speaks the truth.'

In 1520, the intellectual assault against Rome developed alongside another attack which was frankly political in character. This development was the result of the vacuum caused by the death of the Emperor Maximilian. The young man elected at Frankfurt was slow in coming, the Empire remained headless, which opened the way to much speculation. If there were risks to be taken, the right time was before Charles V took up the reins of power. The temptation to confront him on this or that point with a *fait accompli* was so much greater because his youth and inexperience might prevent him from reacting effectively.

The social class most determined to establish its place for the future was that of the knights. It had had its moments of glory, when the robber knights used to swoop down from their eagles' dens to extort a ransom from travellers and cities. They found no resistance to their growing importance except among those of their contemporaries who had remained faithful to the noble ideals of yesteryear. With the development of war and commerce, the knightly class was in decline. The castles, formerly places of happy festivities, were no more than ice-houses where the possibilities of doubtful surprise attacks were gloomily weighed up. The knights lacked an ideology, goals, and a leader to get out of their slump.

Two men were to take it on themselves to remedy this:

Ulrich von Hutten and Franz von Sickingen. The former had escaped from the monastery which the law of primogeniture had obliged him to enter. He had sought his fortune in the service of the Archbishop of Mainz. More a poet than a warrior, he had been the chief author of the *Letters of Obscure Men*. He had dedicated to his master a work on syphilis. He spoke from knowledge of the case, having himself tried all imaginable cures. That sickness had taken on in this age the aspect of a fierce epidemic, a genuine social scourge, which did not spare even the sacred College, and which Julius II's doctor had had to deal with in his patient.

In 1520, Hutten gave vent to his anger. His target was the Roman Church. He raised the standard of nationalism. The Germans would throw off the yoke of the Italians, and Charles V would lead them. Then the matter of Church reform would be taken up: the canons would till the soil like everyone else. Rome would be abandoned to the Turks, with its great worm which was growing fat with food plundered from the whole world. 'Her parasites have sucked our blood, and nibbled our flesh. Now they are attacking the marrow in our bones. . . . To arms! against these plunderers who live from the blood and sweat of the German people, who steal it to pay for slippers, women and favourites in their marble palaces, . . .! When will the Germans understand?'

Rome, for Hutten, was the Pope, the cult of saints, indulgences. One would look in vain there for simplicity, moderation and piety. Too many prostitutes, priests and pen-pushers! They hated nothing so much as the Council, reform and the awakening of the Germans. The answer was: not another penny for Rome, a plain pope, stripped of his parasites, fewer priests and, in any event, fewer of the pseudo-clergy of poor devils and incompetents. And let this whole world be married off to put an end to concubinage! . . .

This was what was being said in Germany from the beginning of April 1520. While Hutten attacked with the pen, Sickingen burnished his weapons with an appropriate military action. He set up his quarters in the ancestral fortress of the Ebernburg, in the Rhineland. He was a warrior, who had served in turn both Francis I and Charles V. At present, he was putting his sword at the service of the knights and the lower nobility.

At the end of this same month of April, contact was made with Luther. He could mobilise single-handed more men than the two knights together. He must be the movement's chaplain. And since he was becoming increasingly less safe, he should come and be installed in the theological fortress, the Ebernburg!

The man concerned did not think for a moment of enlisting in such a crusade. But the question of his safety came up again, as it had at the end of 1518. Information reached him that John Eck was in Rome, and it was not difficult to imagine what he was doing. While everything around him was still calm, Luther had fewer and fewer illusions about what was awaiting him.

The Hussites in Prague had at last heard talk of him, and sent him the works of John Hus, which he did not know, and which he read with increasing surprise. 'We are all Hussites', he said to his friends at Wittenberg. From then on, nearby Bohemia was open to him as a place of refuge.

Luther was in no hurry to reply to the advances of Hutten and Sickingen. He had too much to do. He wrote without stopping. Hutten's theses—German freedom and the destruction of the Roman Curia—were also his. But he had less to say on these subjects than Hutten. His sole objective remained the Gospel.

Besides, he had no need to become Sickingen's vassal. Another knight put at his disposal two hundred armed men. That, after all, would only provide him with a means of intimidation: it would be felt at Rome that it was dangerous to take Luther on physically. The Germans had had enough of the Roman yoke, they were armed and determined; the moment the signal was given, there would be a general conflagration.

16
Leo X

The reports of Charles Miltitz had diverted Leo X's suspicions away from Luther, while the diplomatic manoeuvres over the imperial crown distracted the Pope from dwelling on the news from Germany, that agitation was increasing. Those who did not know of the anxieties of the head of the papal state murmured that the Vicar of Christ showed a scandalous indifference in the face of heresy.

John Eck decided to rekindle the flame. While Commissioner Miltitz was dragging the matter out and making mischief, he, a simple doctor without any authorisation, had taken by storm the position which Luther had sheltered behind since Augsburg. He had granted him the disputation he had wanted and had clarified the whole situation.

Henceforth it was crystal clear that Luther's demand was only a pretence. Even a discussion for some weeks, as equals, had been unsuccessful in persuading him to retract. On the contrary, he had publicly adopted the Hussite heresy and had declared that he no longer believed in the authority of Pope and councils.

The information from the Vice-Chancellor of the University of Ingolstadt and the condemnation pronounced by the University of Cologne at the end of August, made Leo determined to set the proceedings in motion again and, accordingly, Cardinal de Medici took matters in hand.

Eck had become indispensable. He was invited to return to Rome and set off on 18 January, very happy to see his dearest desire realised. While he was waiting, he had to content himself with the services of Miltitz, who was always on the spot. Miltitz was still trying—by what authority was anyone's guess—to make Luther appear before the Archbishop Elector of Trier, and the delivery of the Golden Rose to Frederick the Wise had seemed to him a good opportunity for making a fresh attempt.

The Elector and Luther granted the commissioner the interview which he was seeking, with a good grace. It took place at Liebenwerda, on 9 October. To Miltitz's question about the continuance of the January agreement, Luther replied that nothing had changed. Miltitz imagined that he would be able to lead him off forthwith to Trier, and that thereby he would render a great service to the Elector. Perhaps he hoped to live for a few months at his expense? But they laughed in his face. Frederick intended rather to take Luther with him to the next Diet. However Miltitz soon had his revenge: on 8 December, 1519, he forwarded to the prince a new summons from Rome. If he refused to hand over Luther this time, the Pope would not shrink from excommunication or interdict.

The Elector's council began to be upset by these skirmishes. It was clear to everyone that Rome would not be able to wind up the Luther case on this occasion. No one intended to hand him over. The Elector therefore replied, some months later, that he had always avoided taking a personal position concerning Luther. It was not he, but Miltitz, who had wanted Luther to remain in Saxony, to prevent evil from spreading. Miltitz had boasted so loudly of having designated the Archbishop of Trier as Luther's new judge that no one could impute that to the Elector of Saxony. The commissioner had taken control of the case, and if the result had not been obtained, the blame could only be laid at his door. It was therefore difficult to conceive why the electorate should be struck with excommunication and interdict. The prince had obeyed all the papal orders passed on by Miltitz, and he remained the Holy Father's dutiful son. If Eck, moreover, had not provoked the discussion on the question of the papacy, Luther would not have taken it up. His doctrine, in any case, had so taken root in Germany that the fear of ecclesiastical censures was no longer strong enough

to destroy it. It was necessary rather to oppose it with solid
reasons and Scriptural texts.

The Curia had not waited for this reply before taking up the
case of the crafty ruler, who was from now on as compromised
as his protegé. In a consistory held on 9 January, they branded
the obstinacy, inhumanity and tyranny of this Christian prince
who was for ever fanning a fire that was ready to be put out. In
allying himself with the deadly enemies of the priests and the
Holy See, the Elector had dragged into error the whole Empire,
whose vicar he was. This hydra must be destroyed without
delay. The Pope must give Cardinal Accolti the necessary
power needed to proceed by all canonical means against Luther
and his followers and force them to account for their errors. If
they refused, they should be declared heretics, for the well-
being of religion was at stake. If there were any further delays
in attacking the disease at the roots, the wound would become
incurable.

Leo X was more and more inclined to listen to such advice.
Whatever Luther's errors and merits, the problem went beyond
his person. It was clear that they were faced by one of those
movements which, in the past, had attacked the very substance
of the Church: Arianism in the fourth century, Islam in the
seventh. Luther threatened to combine Arius and Mahomet in
a single person. His doctrine, like that of Arius, misled the
masses, and at any moment he could snatch away entire regions
of Christianity from obedience to the Holy See. Accordingly,
the Pope ordered the renewal of proceedings, not only against
Luther, but equally against Frederick the Wise whose resistance he had to find the means of breaking.

On 1 February, a commission was named, made up of
Observant Franciscans under the presidency of Cardinals
Accolti and Cajetan. Its task was to determine Luther's errors
in detail. As this had just been done by the Universities of
Cologne and Louvain, they were content to vote on the phrases
which had preoccupied these theologians, taking them one
after the other.

This effective but hasty procedure by men of no great competence in the end posed a problem for the best theological head of the whole group: Cajetan. He persuaded the Pope to add about ten theologians to the commission.

In the middle of March they were ready to present Leo with their conclusions: a bull should be published which, without laying the blame on Luther's person, would specifically condemn some of his theses and qualify others according to circumstances as 'scandalous', 'false', 'offensive to pious ears', 'seductive' or 'contrary to Catholic truth'. Luther would be invited by letter to retract. It was not difficult to discern in this proposal the influence of Cajetan who had been clever enough to have appointed some Dominican theologians to support him.

The Pope appeared at first to be satisfied with this result. He ordered Della Volta to press Staupitz again to obtain Luther's retraction. The letter left on 15 March.

But at this moment there arrived in Rome the man who was going to give the matter the direction which it needed: John Eck. The Pope welcomed him with open arms and publicly embraced him. The news from Germany made Leo realise that the situation was becoming more and more serious.

Eck immediately persuaded Leo X to drop Cajetan's plan and to set up a limited committee under the Pope's own direction. The members were Eck, Cajetan, Accolti and a Spaniard, the doctor Johannes. Cajetan was the theologian, Accolti the lawyer. Eck was charged with completing the list of errors cited by the Universities of Cologne and Louvain and approved by Adrian of Utrecht.

On a fine day in May, at the Pope's country seat at Magliana, between two boar hunts, the Vice-Chancellor of Ingolstadt submitted to the sovereign pontiff the new text worked out by the commission. Leo X was delighted. All that was left was to obtain the opinion of the Sacred College which considered it on 21, 23 and 25 May.

It was unanimously agreed that the forty-one theses selected by the commission were worthy of condemnation. The legal aspect of the bull, which was written by Accolti, raised no difficulty, except that Cardinal Carvajal, the former schismatic of Pisa, ineffectually protested against the assertion that the worst of Luther's heresies was that he appealed to the council.

The discussion centred on the precise method to be adopted: the theologians demanded excommunication without qualification on the grounds that Luther's godlessness was sufficiently proven by his books and sermons; but the lawyers asserted that the act itself did not deprive anyone of the right of defending himself for God had accused Adam and Cain before condemning them, and besides the whole matter had begun in 1518 with a summons.

The discussion dragged on: the theologians wanted to have the last word as the guardians of faith and religion; but the lawyers asserted that in sentencing, they alone were competent. What was the good of beginning a legal action vitiated in advance by a structural flaw?

To overcome the dilemma, it was agreed there should be a distinction between three parts of the case: the doctrine, the books and the person. The canonists conceded that the doctrine perhaps could be condemned without need for a charge. But their idea of summoning Luther himself before condemning him was obstinately resisted. The theologians wanted to be able to strike down the guilty one immediately in the name of religion. Finally, they agreed to condemn Luther, but after a certain delay which would take the place of a summons. What to do about the books enflamed the dispute again: the theologians wanted to tie them to the doctrine; the canonists to his person. They couldn't find a solution which satisfied everyone, but they decided to condemn the books and set a day for burning them.

There was more discussion over whether all the books should be burned or only those which contained one or more of the condemned theses. Cajetan asked in vain that each of the suspect propositions be qualified by indicating in what way it was contrary to Church doctrine.

On 1 June the cardinals finally adopted, practically without amendments, the text of the bull which was immediately sent to the Chancellery for editing. By 15 June, it was ready for printing.

The text began with a moving appeal to God and all the saints in heaven: 'Arise, Lord! Vindicate your cause against the fierce foxes who are trying to destroy your vineyard, against the wild boar which wreaks havoc there. . . . Arise, Peter, Paul and all the saints, the Church universal! . . .'

The Pope recalled his endeavours and his patience with Luther: 'In this Roman Curia which he has so much decried on the basis of rumours spread about through ignorance and malice, he had not found very much to blame. We will show him that our predecessors, whose canons and constitutions he has attacked with such violence, have never erred. . . . Despite the bulls of Pius II and Julius II, he has appealed to a future council. . . . We implore him, and his partisans, by the blood of Jesus Christ, to trouble no more the peace of the Church, the unity and truth of the faith, and to renounce error.'

Following an appeal to the German nation, traditionally an ally of the Holy See, forty-one theses of Luther's were condemned. The list was similar to those of the Universities of Cologne and Louvain which served as the basis for the bull. Eck had been able to have added some of Luther's statements at Leipzig:

'It is heretical to assert, as has commonly been the case, that the sacraments confer justifying grace on those who put no obstacle in its path. . . . To deny that sin remains in the child after baptism is to tread under foot both Christ and Saint Paul. . . . The doctrine according to which penitence comprises three parts (contrition, confession, satisfaction) is founded neither in Scripture nor in the holy doctors of Christian antiquity. . . . The best definition of contrition is the proverb: "There is no better penitence than not to begin again, but what is necessary is to change one's life." . . . Those who claim to confess absolutely all their sins want to owe nothing in the end to the mercy of God. . . . Sins are not remitted to him who does not believe; it is not enough that sins are remitted and grace given, one must still believe in the remission. . . . Do not believe that you are absolved on account of your contrition, but by virtue of the words of Christ: "Whatever you remit in my name will be remitted . . ." (Matt. 16.19). Believe in these words and you will be truly absolved, be your contrition as it may. . . . In the matter of the sacrament of penance and the remission of sins, the Pope and the bishop can do no more than the least priest; and even, in the absence of a priest, than any Christian man, woman or child. . . . To approach the sacrament of the Eucharist simply because one has been confessed, because one is conscious of not having committed any mortal sin, and because one has prepared for the communion, is a great error; it is to eat and drink one's own judgement. One must believe on the contrary that one will receive the grace of God by the sacrament itself; it is this faith alone which makes one pure and worthy. . . . It would be a good thing if the Church decided in a council that the laity should communicate in two kinds; the Bohemian Christians who do so are not heretical but schismatic. . . . The treasures of the Church, from which the Pope draws his indulgences are not the merits of Christ and the saints. . . . Indulgences are a pious method of deceiving the faithful and dispensing with the practice of good works; they are the kind of thing which can be useful but are not indispensable. . . . Excommunications are only external punishments which do not deprive a man of the common spiritual prayers of the Church. . . . Christians must be taught to love excommunication, not to fear it. . . . The Roman pontiff, Peter's successor, was not instituted Vicar of Christ for all the Churches in the world: Christ's choice of Peter was not meant in this sense. . . . The word of Christ to Peter "Whatever you shall bind on earth . . ." applied to Peter himself. . . . It is certain that neither the Pope nor the Church can define articles of faith, and still less moral laws. . . . Some articles of John Hus, condemned at the Council of Constance, are very Christian, evangelical and true: The Universal Church cannot reject them. . . . The righteous man sins in every good work. . . . To burn heretics is contrary to the will of the Spirit. . . . War against the Turks is a denial of God's punishment for our sins. . . . No one is sure that he does not constantly commit mortal sins, because of the secret pride of his conscience. . . . Free will after Adam's fall is only an empty word; when man acts, in this sinful condition, he sins mortally. . . . One cannot prove the existence of purgatory on the basis of the authentic books of Scripture. . . . Princes and prelates would do well to put an end to beggary.'

These statements which it would be tedious to give in full were among those which the Roman Church continually rejected in its official teaching, in preaching and the catechism. They showed well how the Roman Catholic tradition kept its distance from Luther's new doctrines. During fifteen centuries of Christian thought and life, convictions had been solidified and customs had been established which were deeply ingrained and which therefore enjoyed unquestioning public support. Moreover, putting all this into question again would entail such a task of analysis and criticism that it would be best not to undertake it. The faithful would lose confidence in the teaching role of the clergy and who could tell if certainties as solid as those questioned would be attained? The bull's authors could not be reproached for not having understood the declarations which they were censuring. In the sense in which they read them, they did not conform with received doctrine and it was perfectly legitimate to react against them.

The weakness of this method was that it excluded all discussion of the condemned doctrine as a whole. Luther's phrases had been taken out of a context which was itself the real question, the only one worth posing. The authors of the condemnation did not seem to be unaware of that fact. But they did not have the courage, or perhaps the skill, to engage Luther in a dialogue which could have transformed a sterile confrontation into an exchange profitable to both parties. The clear evidence of their embarrassment was that whilst they objected precisely to each of the selected theses, they could only describe them in their entirety as 'heretical, false, scandalous, shocking, contrary to Catholic truth'. Once again they dodged Luther's demand that his opponents should speak out openly on the Gospel, rather than on expressions gleaned here and there. He had demanded teaching of substance, but the reply was just confined to a discussion of his real or supposed errors.

The best executed part of the bull was the section relating to sentencing. The canonists had done their work better than the theologians and had forgotten nothing: prohibition of the taking up of Luther's ideas, under pain of excommunication; destruction by fire of the books containing those ideas and prohibition of reprinting, preserving them, or trading in them. Luther and his followers had to retract within sixty days under pain of being declared notorious and obstinate heretics, while the Catholic faithful were forbidden to have the least contact with them. They must be pursued and handed over and every place where they were living must be struck with an interdict. The bull would be published and put into effect everywhere. Anyone contravening these resolutions would be excommunicated.

On the very same day that the Roman Church refused to come to terms with a doctrine it had nurtured in one of its members most attached to the spiritual ideal it wished to promote, the condemned man calmly wrote these lines to a parish priest:

'You ask me how a sermon should be begun and ended. As far as I am concerned, I have never been one for a big introduction. I begin simply: that the Word of God may profit us and that God may favour us, let us first invoke his divine grace and say in silence an Our Father or a Hail Mary. Then I announce the text of Scripture which I want to expound or from which I wish to draw out a lesson. To conclude I say: "That is sufficient for that" or perhaps "We shall return to this point again". Or again, "Having said this, let us pray God to give us the grace to fulfil it". Then comes the ordinary formula for intercession, and Our Father and the benediction. This is my manner of preaching.'

The instrument designed to bring down the man and everything that came from his pen, was ready; but the most difficult thing remained to be done. The administrative system of the time ensured that the guilty man could only be dealt with by the authority on which he directly depended. The bull had to be sent to all the responsible parties. So nothing would be as effective as having on the spot agents who could knock on all the doors and press for the enforcement of the decree, in the name of the Holy See.

The operation was so complex that it was only put into effect in the last half of July. A nuncio was appointed to handle matters with the Emperor and the princes. The task fell to Jerome Aleander, forty years old, a Greek scholar, former rector of the University of Paris and now administrator of the Vatican library. He was given inquisitorial powers, which would permit him to light the bonfires. He could, by the same token, give Luther a safe-conduct if the latter agreed to come to Rome. He was told to avoid any conflict with the other envoy, John Eck, and in any event he should not take the place of the permanent nuncio in Germany, Caracciolo.

John Eck, who was made protonotary for the occasion, was to promulgate the bull in the regions most directly under Luther's influence, and first of all in Saxony. He had the right to add other names to Luther's in the text of the bull. The memory of Leipzig was still too fresh, so all those who had made fun of him there found their way into the bull: Bernard Adelmann, Pirckheimer, Spengler and, of course, the vindictive doctor's other opponent, Karlstadt!

17
The New Mahomet's Koran

The slow progress of the bull did not pass unnoticed. The Saxon principality had an agent in Rome and Luther had been alerted by his correspondents. Before the document had officially left the Curia it had been printed in Germany: someone had stolen a copy of it at the source. Before mid-July, Luther knew all about it and declared 'I almost wish that it would come, this famous bull from Rome which fiercely condemns my doctrine.'

He, too, had crossed his Rubicon. 'From my side, the lot has been cast. I scorn Rome's fury as well as her favours. The time for reconciliation is over, and I want nothing more to do with her. If she condemns me and burns my books, so be it! I will condemn her canon law which is nothing but a tissue of heresies and throw it on the fire. Enough of that humility which has never achieved anything! The enemies of the Gospel should no longer be encouraged in their proud conceit. They chose violence to hide their ignorance and their guilty conscience. . . .'

Frederick had once more received letters from Rome. Being of greater interest to Luther than to him, he faithfully passed them on. He did not want anyone to do a bad turn to his protegé. But this cause was not his, and never would be.

Luther exploded: 'This same injustice and godlessness of Rome! The authorities condemn my books while admitting that they contain much that is spiritual and learned. But they declare that they have never read them nor attempted to read them! My grievances are better founded than theirs. My writings show that

I have been drawn into this affair by a compelling force, not by a quarrelsome disposition. Many a time have I offered peace and proposed silence. I have asked everywhere for someone to show me my error. And I am still ready to be silent if my opponents are reduced to silence.

'Everyone knows that if Eck drew me into a dialogue about papal power, it was solely to dishonour me, my name, everything that is mine, and our university. Since I resisted him, with God's help, I am accused of seeking publicity. But what renown can a man as insignificant as I am have? I have no greater wish than to leave public life and to live in privacy and obscurity.

'Let anyone who wishes take on my job. As long as my professor's chair which confers on me the task of teaching, and declaring God's Word is not taken from me, I remain free to exercise that charge. I already have enough sins on my conscience. I will not add the sin of being silent as long as my job is to teach. I will not let myself be guilty of an impious silence, or of negligence towards the truth or towards thousands of souls.

'I agree entirely that the prince should not identify himself with my cause. . . . Let them punish Prierias, Eck, Cajetan, all those who have without reason unleashed this tragedy on the Roman Church for their own glory. As for me, I am innocent. I acted only when compelled to do so, and I am ready to return to the shadows, provided that no one profits by my silence to stamp out the Gospel. They can have everything that is mine, and I gladly offer it to them, but let them leave Christians free to follow the true path of salvation. This is the one thing which I ask. I want neither a cardinal's hat, nor gold, nor anything which is prized in Rome.

'Only through duty have I adopted this position, which has brought me nothing but difficulty; how can I fear threats, how can promises interest me?'

As he wrote these lines, the situation at Wittenberg was confused enough. The students were agitating, quarrelling with the townsmen. The Elector had forbidden them to carry swords and they were taking no notice. Luther, unable to make his mark in debate, thought he could do so now by a sermon. He was hissed at. A student threatened to throw stones at him. But these incidents scarcely touched him. He had arrived at the point where he was going to say at one go what was on his mind. Already, in debate with the Franciscan, Alveld of Leipzig, he had dealt with the Roman papacy: the organisation created by men under the name of 'the Church' had only an administrative concern. By itself, it was incapable of making Christians. The Church was not a matter of structures. It was above all the brotherhood of those who lived by faith and the Gospel, whatever borders were arbitrarily marked out by the Pope and his excommunications. It had only one leader and one head: Jesus Christ. The papacy was a contingent reality which had nothing to do with faith.

But he had better things to do than to refute the 'Leipzig ass'. At the beginning of August, the printer finished the first copies of a book begun two months earlier and entitled *To the Christian Nobility of the German Nation, concerning the reform of the Christian Estate.*

To be better understood by his public, Luther had abandoned Latin, his usual written language; like Hutten, he now wrote in German. But his audience was not the half-starved knightly class. He addressed himself to the high nobility, and first of all to the Emperor himself, 'the young noble blood which has roused in the heart such great and precious hopes'.

His purpose, as the title indicated, was to invite the German nobility to take up the cause of Church reform. The idea might surprise some, but 'the time for silence was past, the hour for speaking had come'.

The Romans had raised three walls to defend their powers: when called to account by the civil authority they replied that the spiritual power was above the temporal; when texts of Scripture were brought against them, they retorted that the Pope alone had the right to interpret Scripture; and if an appeal were made to a Council, they claimed that it was still for the Pope to decide.

These walls were only paper walls. The clergy's monopoly in so many areas was without foundation. For every Christian was consecrated priest, bishop and pope by his baptism. The sole legitimate hierarchy in society was that of the civil authorities. If the Pope were the only one able to interpret the Scriptures, all Bibles might just as well be burnt! The Christian princes had as much right as the Pope to convoke a council, especially when the deficiencies of the clergy were so obvious to all. Therefore, there was no longer any reason why the Christian nobility should not respond to its vocation and do its duty. Let it convoke a free council, independent of Rome, a council which would free Germany of the Roman yoke.

Luther drew up a programme for this future council. He studied in detail more than twenty questions which most pre-occupied statesmen and popular opinion: reform of the Roman Curia, the clergy and the liturgy; reorganisation of the German Church around the Archbishop of Mainz, assisted by a Synod; financial questions (usury yet again!) and economic questions (restrictions on importing luxuries such as spices and precious materials, which led to a paralysis of trade by reducing the quantity of money in circulation); matrimonial law, etc.

In this great programme, the very radical ideas were mixed with pertinent analyses of the great problems of the day: the Pope would be well served if he were rid of his corrupt Curia; the papal States would be annexed to the Empire, of which they were legally a part; the celibacy of the clergy would be abolished and the sexual instinct would be given respect as as natural a need as drinking, eating and other bodily functions. There would be no more donkeys laden with gold taking the road to Rome.

In issuing what one of his friends called his 'clarion call', Luther certainly reckoned on causing a stir and he was not disappointed. Its impact was tremendous. Four thousand copies were sold in a few days and a new, enlarged edition was immediately sent to press.

Dozens of princes and high-ranking persons sent messages to

the 'Reformer' indicating their approval and gratitude. On the eve of the Diet convoked by the new Emperor, Luther was helping the nobility by providing it with a solid platform for discussion. Whether this Diet would be transformed into a council was another matter.

Even George of Saxony reacted favourably. He wrote to Rome that not everything that Luther had said was false. That these theses should be written down in black and white was not without its uses. 'When no one dares to speak about the evils of the Church, and everyone must be silent, the very stones cry out.'

Many, however, deplored Luther's violence. But it was a calculated violence. Questions dealt with calmly come to grief through indifference. Violence shocks and disturbs, but the judgement of posterity is different from that of contemporaries. Besides, Scripture, as Luther liked to point out, was not opposed to violence among the people of God. Jacob and Esau fought on their mother's breast. The prophets were violent men. Saint Paul called his opponents 'dogs', 'falsely circumcised', 'babblers', 'false workers', 'ministers of satan'. Men are so accustomed to a soothing reading of the Bible that they no longer perceive its brutality.

'Who can say,' Luther declared to his friend Link, 'whether the Spirit is not pressing me vigorously forward?' Always conscious that he was seeking neither glory nor riches (the printers paid him no royalties) nor personal satisfaction, he saw only one motive of which he could be guilty: vengeance. He prayed to God to purify his heart. In any case, he did not wish to provoke sedition, but simply to demand liberty through a General Council.

The *Appeal to the Nobility* was only the first part of the task he had set himself. He had another project and for this he decided to address himself in Latin to the theologians: to unmask the fallacies of Roman dogma.

On 31 August, he announced a new book, dealing with the 'Babylonian Captivity' of the Church. Babylon was the Beast of the Apocalypse, the great harlot—papal Rome. The theme wasn't new, but borrowed by Luther from a copious literary tradition. However, he was to give it a content which exceeded the narrow limits of polemic and raised it to the level of dogmatic principle.

The work appeared on 6 October. Luther assumed that it was only a 'prelude'. Rome was hearing here only the first notes of the tune which he was ready to play. In distinguishing between the Church and the Beast which devours it, he raised the question of the Church's liberation and its reform.

With irony, he explained that because he had been attacked from all sides, he had come to reflect on a great many questions to which he had at first given no thought. The indulgence affair had been only the immediate occasion, and gradually Luther had come to understand that he had at that stage missed the point. What he had written on the subject could now be thrown away.

His conclusion was summed up in a pithy expression which he had printed in capitals:

INDULGENCES ARE JUST A SWINDLE BY THE ROMAN CURIA

He had reflected also on the papacy. It was THE BISHOP OF ROME'S HUNTING GROUND. The Bishop of Rome was not content with his own diocese, but had set up a system of exclusive privileges and powers thanks to which he sponged off the whole world.

But his domination was about to come to an end. It was based on a concept of the sacraments by which he was keeping the Church in slavery. Luther was going to show that the sacraments were not what Rome wanted people to believe.

'I begin by refusing to recognise that there are seven sacraments. For the moment, I retain only three of them: baptism, penance and the bread. They have been brought into a deplorable servitude, and the blame for this is the Roman Curia's. The Church has thus been entirely stripped of its liberty.

'To be true to Scripture, one would have to say that there is only one sacrament and three sacramental signs.'

The unique sacrament in question was the Word of God, which was the sole source of grace for man, and which came to him either directly or under three signs clearly attested by the New Testament: baptism, the eucharist and penance. The four other so-called sacraments: confirmation, orders, marriage and extreme unction were inventions based on misunderstandings.

The three authentic sacraments had been distorted from their true meaning by the papacy. Baptism, which was essentially remission of sins, no longer appeared to have this character, now that so many remedies against sin, such as indulgences, had been invented. But the most serious was the servitude to which the eucharist had been reduced. The words which everyone needed to understand were said in Latin, the chalice was refused to the laity, the dogma of transubstantiation had been invented, and this sacrament had been made a 'sacrifice', the sacrifice of the Mass. Now the fundamental essence of the Mass was the offering of the unique sacrifice of Christ to nourish the faith of believers. Here the function of grace was to strenghen faith by proclaiming the death of the Saviour. The Roman Church had transformed this movement of God towards man into an activity of man towards God. Instead of receiving, man offered. Grace was no longer the source and the fruit of faith, it was to be snatched from God by piling up Masses; hence the mistaken proliferation of private Masses, celebrated by solitary priests who had been ordained only for this purpose. The root of the evil was money: the faithful were induced to turn over sizeable sums of money to have Masses said, and priests were ordained on demand without receiving any instruction.

As for penance, Luther returned to his initial declaration. It was not, perhaps, a sacrament after all, for it lacked a sign as definite as the water of baptism or the eucharistic elements.

This time, the violence was less in the tone of the work than in its thought. Luther did not even ask for the suppression of most of the practices in use. But he tried to change their meaning in a manner so radical that, henceforward, the way was open to a Christianity completely separated from the Roman tradition.

From the purely tactical and immediate point of view, the *Babylonian Captivity* had the effect of depriving the Wittenberg doctor's opponent of his most formidable weapon. For three years, Rome had been accusing Luther of deviating from Catholic truth, of which it alone was judge. The much-vaunted orthodoxy of Rome was shown to be a pretence, which could not stand up to confrontation with the spirit and letter of Scripture.

Rome or Scripture: this alternative, according to Luther, was thrust upon every Christian conscience in such a way that he was going to propound it to the Pope himself, to Leo X, the 'poor lamb', the Daniel in the den of Roman lions!

The opportunity was given to him by the inimitable Miltitz, who now made a final appearance on the scene. He was fired perhaps by a desire to leave to posterity a lasting result of his efforts. At all events, his final initiative drew from Luther the best of his trumpet-blasts: *The Liberty of the Christian.*

Rome seemed to have forgotten its commissioner for some time and he himself realised that his career was seriously compromised. The bull of condemnation clearly showed that his inquiries of the previous year were no longer appreciated in high places. But perhaps it was still possible to save the situation by taking up again the notion of reconciling Luther with the Pope.

Frederick the Wise was also very anxious for an arrangement. He was waiting in Cologne for the imminent arrival of the Emperor and he was uneasy. He was going to be relieved of his functions as imperial Vicar by the pressure of events and he knew that the nuncios were actively at work with his Imperial Majesty to get the bull enforced. Once Luther was defeated, they would once more turn against him.

For the moment, Miltitz was the sole means of action at the disposal of Saxon diplomacy. His status as representative of Rome had indeed lost something of its lustre, but one could still turn it to account. . . .

So it was that, on 11 October, at 4 o'clock in the afternoon,

Luther stopped off at the Antonite priory of Lichtenberg on the Elbe, half-way between Wittenberg and Leipzig. Von Feilitzsch had seen to it that he was accompanied by four bodyguards. Just by the meeting place, thirty other armed men were posted; the commissioner should not be tempted to settle the matter by the most expedient way!

But Miltitz was far from harbouring such designs. Favourably disposed as ever towards Luther, he had found a new scape-goat: John Eck. Miltitz was returning from the Leipzig rumpus, where he had met the man who had supplanted him in Rome's favour, having brought all his efforts to nothing.

Miltitz had to outstrip the man with the bull who was promulgating it in the region and had just brought it to Wittenberg. Before the sixty-day period of delay granted to Luther ran out, the latter would draw up a brief account of his doctrine for the Pope, and add to it a respectful and conciliatory letter. Miltitz would bring the whole thing to the Holy Father by hand.

Luther promised everything, even silence. His obstinacy in doctrinal matters was equalled only by his submissiveness in yielding to the schemes of the Saxon court. Miltitz was so pleased with the result of the interview that he accompanied Luther on the road to Wittenberg. He remembered to ask the Elector for frequent consignments of his 'image' (the one struck on pieces of money) since he had some good friends at Rome who had become cardinals, and he could do nothing empty-handed.

Luther had no difficulty in putting on paper the ideas which he wanted to communicate to Leo X. For a long time, he had been waiting for the Pope to pronounce directly on the doctrine which he, Luther, found in Scripture, instead of hounding him on account of the inferences which his enemies professed to draw out of it.

Once and for all, his position was as follows:

The sole means of grace granted to men was the Word of God. To that appeal which touched the conscience in its very depths, there was one response: faith. 'Faith is the sole work which God requires.' From that point on, no law was imposed on the believer. He was free. Works were born of love and did not need to be prescribed. The framework to which the Church subjected the believer was comparable to the scaffolding from which the cathedral rose up. Luther had the impression that the Roman Church had made the structure an end in itself which developed and increased each day, while inside there was nothing.

Two days were enough to put the finishing touches on this *Treatise on Christian Freedom*. The letter which was to accompany it was already prepared. Luther slated all his opponents and tried to induce Leo X to dissociate himself from his Roman Curia and even from the papacy. He offered him a course of reflection on the true Christian life, and said how glad he would be if they could end their days discussing together the Word of God and faith.

Charles Miltitz was in fact unable to recover his position with this mixture of gall and honey. The printing of the texts, of which Luther had edited two versions, one in Latin for the Pope, the other in German for the people, took longer than expected. When the commissioner received them, it was too late. So much had happened in between that no one could believe that the plan would succeed. Miltitz receded into the background with his precious documents. Perhaps they would enable him to maintain his position while he waited for another opportunity. At all events, his name remained inseparable from the greatest bookselling success which had yet issued from Luther's pen.

18
Nuncio Aleander's Cross

Charles I, King of Spain, was in Barcelona when he was told that he had become Charles V, Emperor of Germany, King of the Romans, successor of Charlemagne ... heady titles for a twenty-year old boy, whose teachers had nurtured in him a vision of the world straight out of the tales of chivalry.

But the Don Quixote of the family was dead. That was his grandfather, Maximilian. He had almost married the Duchess Anne, and in fact the contract had been signed. But Louis XII, who was thought to be already married, had tricked the Hapsburgs out of Brittany by marrying the widow of Charles VIII of France, with the Pope's approval. Nothing daunted, Maximilian had then sought to have himself named papal coadjutor, with the right of succession to the triple crown.

The fact was that madness was in Charles' family. He was only regent of Spain: the titular sovereign was his mother, mad Joanna, who was kept well under guard; and she had her supporters who were hostile to the little Burgundian king.

Burgundy! the splendid Empire of Charles the Bold (another one who wanted to make himself pope!), placed seductively between the Jura and the North Sea. ... Charles spoke only French fluently. Civilisation, for him, was the refined environment of the Burgundian court, a splendid and easy-going life, the life of ceremony.

He had only just become Spanish and must now become German. That meant, first of all, that he had to leave Spain, where his power was still precarious, to put on the crown of an empire where he was but a stranger.

On 20 May, 1520, he embarked at Corunna for Antwerp,

since his conflict over the duchy of Burgundy made France a less secure route than the ocean. The Spanish fleet had extended the world's frontiers. Since 1492, gold had flowed in from the new lands discovered by the Genoese sailor, Christopher Columbus—gold, the keystone of an empire on which the sun never set.

From Molino del Rey, on 31 October 1519, Charles had written his first letter to the German States. By stages he meant to reach Aachen, Charlemagne's capital, the traditional place of coronation. From there, the imperial court would proceed up the Rhine to Worms, where the first Diet of his reign would be held.

On his arrival at Antwerp, the man who was already called 'Emperor' realised that his difficulties were only just beginning. The nuncio Caracciolo, who spoke again of a crusade against the Turks, was soon joined by the nuncio Aleander, who was in charge of the crusade against Luther.

Charles had no taste for doctrinal innovations. The inflexible Adrian of Utrecht, whom he had made Archbishop of Tortosa and for whom he had obtained a cardinal's hat, had brought him up in a Catholicism opposed to all dogmatic experiment (and not too keen on emotionalism). Father Glapion, his Franciscan confessor, was careful to keep him in a good humour.

Aleander easily persuaded Charles to decree the destruction of Luther's books in his hereditary states of Flanders and Burgundy. But as far as Germany was concerned, nothing could be decided before the coronation. On 8 October at Louvain and on the 15th at Liège, the first bonfires were lit.

Leaving this unhappy trail behind him, the blond youth at last set foot on his empire's soil. The princes had come to welcome him. He received in total silence the dutiful compliments, the homage, the smiles and promises. This was taken for shyness. But he had only done what was expected of him: no one had a very exalted idea of the abilities, intellectual or not, of this frail young man who looked so awkward in the robes of his proud counsellors, like a young noble in his chaperone's skirts. He did not even consider it worthwhile to bother with conversation, even though he was among princes who spoke French, such as the Elector Frederick.

After the coronation ceremony which took place on 23 October, under the arches of the Church of the Three Wise Kings, Aleander returned to the attack. The King of the Romans had sworn to maintain and promote the Holy Catholic faith and to be the faithful servant of the Church. Would he now sign the decree which would make it possible to begin the purge in Germany?

The imperial counsellors were against it. The reign should not begin with a show of force and still less by a trial of strength. The Emperor should first of all take over the reins from the hands of the imperial Vicar, who was waiting for him at Cologne.

Aleander began to sense what was waiting for him. His colleague, John Eck, was already ruined. He had been able to have the bull posted in September at Meissen, Merseburg and Brandenburg. But the University of Leipzig, which had given him such a victory only the year before, would have nothing to do with it. From Leipzig, he had sent the document to the University of Wittenberg which had received it on 3 October. The rector, Peter Burkhard, had evaded his obligation of enforcing the decree, arguing that Eck had not transmitted the bull in due form. To gain time, he had sent it to the Elector, that is to say, to Cologne, and he awaited orders. At Erfurt, Torgau, Döbeln, Freibourg, Magdeburg, he had no success, and it was the same in Vienna. In his own town, Ingolstadt, Eck had the very greatest difficulty in imposing the papal will.

Luther, who was preparing to publish the *Babylonian Captivity*, was, one suspects, not in the least affected. 'I despise this bull,' he wrote on 13 October to Spalatin. 'I attack it as the blasphemous and lying thing that it is . . . the spitting image of Eck!' He quickly disposed of it. Basically, it was a condemnation of Christ himself, which meant it had no influence over him.

To the doctrinal conflict in progress it brought no proof at all—
it was a pointless exercise! There was nothing to do but fight it,
and first by putting its authenticity in doubt. Prince Frederick
could pretend to ignore it: at Leipzig and elsewhere, it had
become the object of general scorn; to concern himself with it
would be to do it too much honour. Left alone, it would burst
like a soap bubble.

The Emperor was the greatest unknown factor. Luther did
not believe he was the man to act with the same freedom which
Luther himself had pioneered. Erasmus had warned him, from
Cologne, that the court was full of friars. You could not count
on Charles. Scripture, moreover, advised against putting trust
in princes, for there was no salvation in them.

At Cologne itself, which was for some weeks the capital of the
Holy Roman Empire, there was much talk of Luther. All those
who wished to gain something from the first meeting with their
new master had flocked there: princes, nobles, dignitaries of all
kinds, merchants, of course, and above all humanists. Even
Erasmus came to try his luck. Everyone was plotting and the
Luther case was not least among the subjects for discussion.

Aleander arrived on 29 October in the city of Albert the
Great and Duns Scotus, whose graves still mark today the
collapse in the thirteenth century of the prescholastic scriptural
theology which Luther so admired. The nuncio met general
hostility. The Elector of Saxony, to whom he attempted to
present the bull against Luther officially, obstinately refused to
receive him or his colleague Caracciolo, the other nuncio. The
humanists waged a fierce battle against the Hellenist who had
gone over into the obscurantist camp. Rumours were circulated
about him: he was a Jew not validly baptised, which would
explain why he had become a pimp for the Roman courtesans,
and a friend of Italian sodomites.

Frederick's piety, however, allowed the nuncios to trap the
old fox outside his lair. On 4 November, they caught him in the
middle of Mass, and presented him with a letter from the Pope
and the bull, indicating to him that he no longer had any choice

but to have Luther's books burned and to deliver up the heretic. They boasted of having the agreement of the Emperor and the princes.

The Elector replied that this was neither the time nor the place for dealing with such a matter and, on the following day, he called in Erasmus for his advice. The great man began by observing that Luther went a little too far. But in principle he was still won over to a movement on whose behalf he had intervened many times. Erasmus' international reputation gave him the right to take sides, even against the Curia; but he chose to keep his peace.

Frederick and Spalatin, however, were looking for solid support against the growing threat. Erasmus of Rotterdam must communicate his caution to Luther. The learned scholar tried to dodge the issue with a frivolous paradox: 'Luther has committed unpardonable errors, touching on the papal crown and the monks' bellies.'

By pressing him, they persuaded him to write down the judgements he could make in Luther's favour. These *Axioms* comprised the first important consideration given to the thought and intentions of the Wittenberg monk.

The campaign against Luther seemed to Erasmus to spring from hatred of classical studies and from power motives. 'Good Christians, those of truly evangelical spirit, are less shocked by Luther's principles than by the tone of the papal bull. Luther is right to ask for impartial judges. The world is thirsting for evangelical truth, and it is unjust to oppose such praiseworthy aspirations with so much hatred. The Emperor would be ill-advised to begin his reign over-rigorously. The Pope is seeking to promote his own cause more than the glory of Jesus Christ. Luther has still not been refuted and his opponents' writings have nowhere been approved. The matter should be entrusted to men who are intelligent and above all suspicion. The Emperor is a prisoner of papists and sophists.'

To get involved as far as this was not Erasmus's nature. He insisted on reconsidering his text the next day. 'See with what courage Erasmus prepares to confess the Gospel' said Spalatin ironically. But there had been time to take a copy of the *Axioms* and they had been printed. Erasmus no longer knew where to stand.

The nuncio successfully discouraged him from playing further with fire. The scholar had taken the liberty of expressing some doubts on the authenticity of the bull. It owed so much to Cologne and Louvain that one could legitimately suspect that the Grand Inquisitor of Cologne, Hoogstraten, was no stranger to it. It would not be the first time that an apocryphal bull was circulated. Ever since Lorenzo Valla had denounced the forgery of the Donation of Constantine, according to which the ancient Emperor Constantine had made the Pope his heir, intellectuals were suspicious. Aleander in turn summoned Erasmus and put in his hands an authentic copy of the document. Erasmus was at a loss. It was the end of the power he had so carefully and happily exercised until then over the minds of men and the movement of ideas. Aleander would not forgive him, while Luther would repudiate the master in whom he had discerned for some time a greater love of man than of God. Erasmus could have been the Reformer, and he himself had imagined that the Church would have no other deliverer but him. He was more gifted, more balanced than Luther. He had compromised himself just as much on many points. But as *The* Reformer said, 'He had pulled his neck out of the noose.'

In the end, Frederick left Cologne. As soon as he turned his back, Aleander took advantage of his absence to have Luther's writings thrown on the fire. But neither the Prince–Bishop nor the chapter, nor the municipal council, nor even the university would countenance an execution, even though it was approved by the Emperor. The nuncio had to be content with a surreptitious bonfire—all the more absurd because, unknown to him, watchful hands had substituted for the heretical books papers of no value at all! And even that was an improvement on the bonfire in Louvain, where the students had palmed off on an illiterate executioner a heap of catholic works!

The same thing happened at Mainz, but this time the executioner considered the task beneath his dignity. He knew his job and said he was bound to burn only what had been condemned by a tribunal. Now this was not the case with Luther's writings: the bull had still not been officially promulgated. However, the Archbishop came to the assistance of the nuncio, but the students here too fed the fire with the works of the 'victim's' opponents. Despite all this, Aleander believed that he noticed a change in public opinion: men were impressed by the determination of the Roman representatives.

The only drawback was that this process could be used by your opponent to the same advantage and this was what they were talking about doing at Wittenberg. At the beginning of December, Spalatin came across Luther making a stack of folios: canon law, decretals, summae. A copy of the bull was also ready to undergo its fate. The Elector who had not forgiven the burning at Cologne was in agreement.

On the 10th, the Wittenberg students who had risen early read the following, posted on the Church door: 'Let all those who are bound to the study of the Gospel of truth be present at 9 o'clock, at the chapel of the Holy Cross outside the walls. In conformity with ancient apostolic usage, the impious books of scholastic theology and pontifical law will be burnt. For the enemies of the Gospel have been so audacious as to burn the truly evangelical books of Luther. Come! faithful and studious young men, do not miss this sacred spectacle! Perhaps the hour has come for unmasking the Antichrist.'

Much less than this would have drawn a crowd. 'Fuel' was collected from the town. However, some students were careful not to surrender their copies of Saint Thomas's *Summa* or Duns Scotus's *Commentary on the Sentences*.

The place chosen was the place of execution, the town 'dump'. Before an audience composed entirely of professors and students, Gratian's *Decretum*, the *Decretals*, the *Sextus*, the *Clementines*, the *Extravagantes*, the *Summa* of Angelo Chiaviasso, Eck's *Chryso-passus*, the books of Emser and other contemptible characters disappeared in flames. Luther then came forward and threw a little volume on the fire declaring: 'Because you have destroyed the Lord's truth, may the Lord destroy you today in the fire!' Some Amens were said. Then the professors withdrew, leaving the students to improvise what followed.

The next day, in front of an audience of four hundred, Luther explained: 'You no longer have the choice between hell and the stake.' And to Spalatin 'I wanted to show the incendiary papists that it was easy for them to burn the books which they couldn't refute.' He had given Aleander a dose of his own medicine.

On 28 November the Emperor arrived at Worms, along with his court and, while waiting for the opening of the Diet, scheduled for January, he travelled around the surrounding country on horseback.

The nuncio Aleander's first problem was to find lodgings. The citizens of Worms did not pelt him with stones like those of Mainz, but he was refused entry to the lodgings rented for him. He offered to pay more, but to no purpose. In the end, he had to take refuge in a little room without a chimney, let by a man too poor to take his opposition to extremes. The banks of the Rhine were cold at this time of the year, and the poor librarian dreamt sadly of his well-warmed study where he had been working in comfort from September to May. To be sure, his host invited him to come and warm himself in the boiler room. But the filthiness, the cramped nature of the room and the smoke made him prefer the risk of cold. He wondered what he would do if he became ill.

There was a rumour that Hutten and his friends had sworn to assassinate him. The Bishop of Liège had advised him, on behalf of the princes and the imperial court, to be on his guard. It was feared that he might not leave Germany alive. Indeed he felt less safe than in the Roman countryside, which was saying quite a lot.

Luther seemed to be off the leash. Even before his outrage

against papal rights was heard of at Worms new writings arrived, each more aggressive than the last. One was entitled *Against the Bull of the Antichrist*:

'Pope Leo, Lord Cardinals, all you who have some power in Rome, I openly declare to you that if this Bull is from you, I, in the full authority of a child of God and fellow heir with Jesus Christ, leaning on this rock and without fear of hell, advise you in the name of the Lord to commune with yourselves, to cease your blasphemies, and quickly. Otherwise, know that I and all the servants of Jesus Christ will henceforth consider your papal throne as occupied by Satan and as the seat of the Antichrist, which we do not choose to obey; on the contrary, we ask you never again to absolve us and to end your bloody tyranny over us.'

On 17 November the heretic had renewed his appeal to a future General Council, treating the Pope as a dishonest, obdurate heretical and apostate judge. Another book explained *Why the Writings of the Pope were burned by Doctor Luther*.

But the nuncio could no longer hold back the avalanche. He could not renew his incendiary feats, for, he wrote to Rome, 'a legion of desperate men under Hutten's banner is thirsty for priests' blood and is looking only for the opportunity of overthrowing us.' Moreover, a new front had just opened up: the Elector of Saxony had asked the Emperor to summon Luther to the Diet and the Emperor had agreed.

That decision was as damaging to the Pope as the *Babylonian Captivity*. It amounted to a clear assertion that temporal power was not subject to spiritual power. For no one had the right to reopen a case judged by the Pope. Since the Pope had issued the condemnation, the Emperor had only to carry it out.

Charles V, to be sure, was not to blame. This kind of matter rested entirely with his counsellors: Charles-Guillaume de Croy, Lord of Chièvres, his chancellor Gattinara and his confessor, the French Franciscan Glapion. Chièvres had not forgotten Leo's campaign on behalf of Francis I and he was so indispensable to the young Emperor that they slept in the same room.

Aleander played a decisive part, not so much in Luther's condemnation, as in support of papal primacy. He had to prevent the sovereign pontiff's authority, defied by Luther and his followers, from being eroded by the new Emperor at the very beginning of his reign. The way to counter this danger was to obtain from the imperial government an 'edict', that is to say a decree publicly imposing the bull.

Two weeks after the Emperor's agreement with the Elector of Saxony, the nuncio managed to convince Chièvres and Gattinara that Luther could not be summoned before having recanted. And even then he should not set foot in Worms, since his presence would bring with it the interdict on the city. He should remain at Frankfurt or Oppenheim, awaiting the decision on his fate.

It was on 17 December then that the Emperor rescinded his decision. But his letter to Frederick crossed with a message from the Elector which said that he was withdrawing his request. He demanded that Luther should appear before impartial judges and protested against the fact that his books had been burnt without imperial authorisation. Whatever the motives for this about turn, the Elector's previous idea of bringing Luther to the Diet himself was clearly buried. The way was open for a new initiative.

As could be expected, it came from the nuncio. At Aleander's request the permanent council, representing the German States at the imperial court, transformed the bull on 29 December into an immediately enforceable law of the Empire. All that was necessary was to give the decision the seal of the High-Chancellor—the Archbishop of Mainz—and ... to obtain the consent of Frederick the Wise!

Albert of Brandenburg hesitated to sign it. While waiting for his decision, Aleander drew up instructions for the two envoys which the permanent council wanted to send to the Elector of Saxony. He lined up all the arguments that could finally remove the protection Frederick gave to Luther.

The ambassadors would have to speak to the prince in the absence of his counsellors, who were more Lutheran than Luther. They were to present themselves as envoys of his Imperial Catholic Majesty and appeal for the protection of religion, faith and Christian unity. They should not forget to praise the prince's piety and the faith of his ancestors. He should no longer be guided by resentment against churchmen, 'for that bears no comparison with what our ancestors handed down to us, that is to say, sacraments, rites, ceremonies, and the whole structure of the Catholic faith.' There was nothing which Christ forbade more strictly than revolt and division. If the popes sin, they have a judge in heaven. Christ had never said that the pope could be deposed, driven out or put to death. Men invested with authority could sin and often did. But their authority was not thereby abrogated and always deserved respect. It was unheard of and insane that a simple monk should judge and condemn popes, when he himself said that neither the pope nor any other man should judge or condemn, or even to proclaim the slightest law without the free consent of those below.

In this way Luther abolished all obedience and all rule. If he still aimed only at the clergy, this was so as not to stir up the princes against him. But once piety and priestly authority, which is given by divine right, had been destroyed, it would be easy for him to overturn secular authority which was not even based on natural law. No one would respect the secular sphere who had scorned the sacred! Luther overturned all laws, and he would have legislated for civil society if he were not more fearful of the Emperor's sword than of papal excommunication.

Bad popes were nothing new. But it was a pope who had consecrated Pepin the Short King of the Franks and Charlemagne Emperor. The Pope had transferred the Eastern Empire to the Franks, from the Franks to Germany and had granted the imperial election to the Germans alone. If papal authority were annulled, if all men were equal, if for centuries there was no true pope, then there was no longer an empire or emperor, or electoral princes. . . .

Leo X's person was not open to attack. His election had been free of simony, and his conduct beyond reproach. The abuses of the Curia were fewer in number and less serious than the Germans supposed. Moreover, it was always possible for the Emperor to ask Rome to reform itself.

The Lutherans boasted of being the most faithful sons of the Catholic Church, but they didn't want to hear a word about the Roman Church or the Holy See. If they alone possessed the Catholic faith, were Christians who obeyed the Holy See therefore misguided? Was it reasonable to think that for so many centuries, so many men of genius and character had been deceived and that the Holy Spirit had abandoned the Church? The truth was that Luther and his followers had separated themselves from the Church and made a schism. It was not we who had separated ourselves from them.

The envoys of his Imperial Majesty had not come to count Luther's errors, which were beyond number. They would allow themselves neither to read nor to touch the books condemned by the Apostolic See. They would simply ask the prince what he thought of Luther who had burned papal decrees and condemned the Council of Constance. Had the entire world been in error until this moment, and was Luther the only one to see what was right? Didn't this enormity in itself show that Luther was the most wicked and impious of arch-heretics?

The envoys were to reply also to the prince's usual objections asking whether Luther had been provoked by his opponents and whether you could burn his books before you had heard and been convinced by a disputation. 'A fine defender of the life of the Gospel who, to avenge himself on his opponents, tramples the Catholic faith underfoot!' What purpose was to be served in having Luther present at Worms? His books were in everyone's hands. They were a precise and more solid basis than any discussion. Saint Jerome said that there was no need of an inquiry when the blasphemy was notorious. And, moreover, before what judges should he be made to appear? The theologians and lawyers? He had burned their books. The philosophers? He had described their prince, Aristotle, as an animal. The bishops? He wanted to abolish their dignity and their authority. How, and by what authority could he be convinced? Learning, the professions or books?: he condemned them all.

Many competent men were ready to enter the arena with him. But they did not wish to appear to debate about the authority which the Pope had received from God and which had been recognised for so many centuries by the emperors and the people. Luther should not be allowed to debate on the ceremonies, and on the Catholic faith sanctified by the oracles of the prophets, the witness of the apostles, the blood of martyrs and the teaching of the doctors.

The envoys of his Imperial Majesty should appeal to Frederick's sense of authority: Luther was a rebellious and seditious subject. They should talk only very carefully of excommunication and the interdict. They should show that an appeal to a future council was ineffectual, worthless and unreasonable, dangerous for the plaintiff and his protectors. They should touch on the matter of the sacraments.

Finally, they should ask the Elector to make Luther understand that a retraction on his part—which he had previously promised—would be entirely honourable and would earn his pardon.

In any event, the prince must be begged to put a stop to the evil. The purpose of the mission was to get him to order the destruction of Luther's books and to keep him in a safe place pending the Emperor's decision. He should not fear the people: the people copied their superiors' conduct and would give up lost causes.

To sum up: they should insist on the Emperor's authority and his determination, on the fact that the Empire could not exist without the Roman Church, on the inappropriateness of a hearing for Luther himself when it was his writings which were in question. They should call to mind the Pope's wisdom and goodwill from the start. The case before Cajetan was still pending and that could present a procedural difficulty; but Cajetan had not received a commission, properly speaking.

The nuncio formally opposed Luther's coming to Worms: they had his books and this was enough. Moreover, if Luther were condemned, he would reject his judges. And if he had a safe-conduct nothing could be done against him. He would do as he did in Augsburg: retract in conversation and the next day withdraw his retraction before the notary.

Thus Aleander masterfully summed up the policy whose success it was his mission to ensure. Luther's doctrine could not be accepted by the Roman Church. It offended grievously everything which conscience held most dear and sacred. His objective was to stamp out this doctrine and destroy the books which contained it. The most decisive blow would be for its author to deny it. But he could manage without Luther's retraction. There was a bull, an imperial law had just been adopted which made its application possible, and there was hope that the Elector of Saxony's opposition could now be overcome. Nothing could now prevent him from ridding Germany and Christianity of its 'poison'.

As for Luther himself, the essential thing was to prevent him from doing any harm, one way or the other. His intentions did not matter. The question of his innocence or guilt was quite distinct from the problem posed by his doctrine. The nuncio was not empowered to institute proceedings against a person, but to implement a decision against a patently obvious heresy. Luther should not come to Worms. This was the best way of avoiding confusion.

So by different paths, the Roman representative had arrived at the same conclusion as Luther: that only doctrine matters. Whatever part was played by personal factors in Luther's violent assaults, there was no doubt that because of the pressure exerted for three years to stamp out his teaching he had hardened his attitude. He no longer sought a 'trial of Luther'.

But Aleander made the mistake of underestimating a factor of major importance. According to German public opinion, the doctrine attacked was one of those which must be defended. And the man most suited to defend it was a champion who had proved his capability. Germany would not allow Lutheranism to be separated from Luther.

Moreover, circumstances cut short the nuncio's offensive. The Elector of Saxony arrived at Worms on 5 January, before the delegation was ready and before the High-Chancellor had put the edict into effect. Frederick dashed into the Emperor and asked for an explanation. He was in a position of strength, as there was some embarrassment about having annulled an imperial favour to an electoral prince. He got them to agree that Luther would be heard and that force would not be used.

Informed of this, Luther replied that he was ready to go to Worms, but he would do so to discuss his doctrine freely with men competent in Holy Scripture.

19
The Battlefield of Worms

On 3 January 1521, Pope Leo X signed a new bull, his last: the period of grace given Luther to retract had expired and he was declared an 'obstinate heretic' and excommunicated. Everywhere he stayed was put under an interdict, which meant suspension of the liturgy. His associates, especially Hutten, suffered the same penalties. All that remained was to have the sentence published everywhere by the bishops. The religious orders were to be used to get the sentence recognised and to defend it.

As with the preceding bull, the problem was to obtain the necessary counter-signatures of the secular authorities. The nuncios were instructed to appoint inquisitors who could appeal to the secular arm. On 18 January, the Pope wrote to ask the Emperor to have the judgement against the new heretic published and to make sure that it was fully carried out by an edict.

This new escalation on Rome's part had been requested by Aleander. It had the disadvantage, just then, of Luther bringing himself back into the foreground before having finished with his doctrine. The other excommunicates, driven into a corner, were inevitably going to combine with Luther, for his fall would doubtless be followed by their own execution.

But for a moment it seemed that Rome had scored a point. The Emperor then and there tore to pieces a message from Luther brought him by a high Saxon functionary. Aleander, who recovered the fragments for the Vatican library, hurried to send off the good news to Rome: his Majesty was in high humour.

The Diet began officially on 28 January. Its agenda included, among other items, the question of the money and troops which the Emperor needed to get himself crowned in Italy by the

Pope, and the perennial item, the *Grievances of the German Nation* against the Roman Curia. Luther was not on the programme. The matter was being dealt with at the Chancellery, where the Emperor had ordered the preparation of a German translation of the edict.

However, the Diet members made their feelings in favour of Luther felt in a disturbing fashion. So much so that the imperial counsellors willingly agreed to a suggestion made by Father Glapion which, if successful, would make it possible to avert a clash with the powerful Lutheran party. The French Franciscan, newly arrived at the court, had the twofold advantage of being a private person yet with access to the Emperor. He suggested he should make a private approach to the Elector Frederick, in the name of the Emperor. The nuncios, who were kept informed, realised that control was being taken out of their hands, but they made no objection. Doubtless Aleander remembered that he had once thought of a similar approach.

Glapion was among those who had read Luther's first writings with enthusiasm. He had believed in the Wittenberg Gospel and still did, but he thought that Luther had dealt a fatal blow to his cause by his inexcusable *Babylonian Captivity*. Yet he still hoped that Luther would put the matter straight and resume his providential role within the Church.

The imperial confessor's application for an audience with the Prince of Saxony met with a categorical refusal. Frederick spoke French well, but he had nothing to say. The most he could agree to was to authorise his chancellor, Brück, to meet Glapion. The Franciscan presented the chancellor with a list of errors which he had noticed in the *Babylonian Captivity*.

'But,' he commented, 'no evil was without a cure, not even the evil caused by this book. Luther could easily make amends by retracting. Besides, he was not obliged to contradict himself in order to do this: the world only wanted to believe that these passages which contradicted to such an extent his earlier writings were not written by him.'

Brück had his reply ready. He let the confessor enumerate

the other loopholes he had thought out: namely to admit that Luther had gone to excess in conducting his legitimate defence, or, again: to say that he understood the quoted passages only in a sense that conformed to the teaching of the Roman Church. Then he snapped,

'Reverend Father, the *Babylonian Captivity* has nothing to do with the matter. The bull came before it, and condemns precisely the doctrine which you yourself find beyond reproach.'

'No matter. If Luther denies his *Captivity* one way or the other, I am sure that the Pope will take up the dialogue with him, and some account will be taken of his requests. He wants a commission to arbitrate, and the Emperor will name one composed of impartial and enlightened men. It will meet behind closed doors and of course at a time more opportune than now. Until then, the two parties would observe a truce; Luther's books would be sequestered, but burning of them would cease. Why should his Highness not put such a request to the Emperor? . . .'

'His Highness' replied that he could not decide in Luther's place! With a heavy heart, the eminent old man gave up the struggle. He was soon to be sent to finish his days in South America. . . .

Glapion had naturally informed his penitent of his approach, and of its failure. Charles then decided to turn the matter back to the nuncio. On Shrove Tuesday, he asked him to speak to the Diet the following day. Aleander understood only too well how high the stakes now were. The situation was getting worse and worse: the Lutherans were actively opposing in the Diet the publication of the edict against Luther. The nuncio frequently came across men who, on seeing him, instinctively put hand to sword. Everyone was reading Luther's writings. Portraits depicted him with a halo. A tract dedicated to Luther and Hutten bore the inscription: 'To the front-line fighters for Christian liberty.' Rumours went about that Luther had been offered a cardinal's hat. . . . In short, in the little imperial capital of the moment, the spell was complete.

To strengthen his position, the nuncio bombarded the Curia with suggestions. They must hasten to suppress abuses, and above all they should not provoke the Germans. There should never have been such a long delay. Some years before, the Vatican prefect had warned the Pope: 'It would need only the rantings of a fool to unleash the full force which has built up against Rome.' The Emperor and each of the princes should forthwith be sent favours, money and letters. Rome must show strong evidence of its determination to encourage the faithful and overawe the opposition.

So, Leo X sent a letter to Charles V telling him that he thanked God for having given the Church such an Emperor (fear had made him forgetful). . . . And, while his representative at Worms risked his life to defend his throne, the Pope was entertained by the buffooneries of the Roman carnival. Under his window, in the courtyard of the Castel Sant'Angelo, a stage had been set up. The performance began with a woman praying to Venus, asking for a lover. Soon, the drums rolled and eight monks, dressed in grey serge, rolled onto the stage dancing a *sarabande* around the personification of Love. They beat her unmercifully and she defended herself somehow with her quiver. A little later, the Holy Father saw Love in turn pleading with Venus to save her from the monks who had taken her bow. The goddess then told the woman to approach. Provided with a magical drink, Love managed to put the monks to sleep. They were awakened by arrow shots from Love. Totally spellbound, they beset the woman with declarations of love, threw off their cowls and began to fight among themselves, the victor obtaining her hand.

The Diet would not forgive the nuncio if he tried playing a part. His speech was ready and was to last three hours.

On Ash Wednesday, there was but one absentee from the full ranks of the Diet: Frederick the Wise. Aleander began by establishing that Luther could not be allowed to attack the Pope. Since gentle ways had not worked, there remained only one solution: to put him under the imperial ban. This measure carried risks, but there was no choice. Besides, the new party was just a rabble of impertinent men of letters, decadent clerics, ignorant lawyers, ruined nobles and bribed paupers. Strength, power, wisdom, and reason were all on the other side. Putting Luther under the imperial ban would open everybody's eyes. 'Beware lest the Lutheran heresy bring Germany into subjection as the abominable and impudent doctrine of Mahomet has subjected Asia.'

Charles V immediately accepted the nuncio's proposition, and wanted to publish the edict putting Luther under the imperial ban. But his counsellors decided it was impossible and dangerous to make a move without consulting the Diet. The Diet may indeed have welcomed the nuncio's speech, but the Lutherans were not beaten yet.

The Diet deliberated for a whole week. Passions became so heated that the Electors of Brandenburg and Saxony fell on each other, and were only just separated in time. No one had seen such a thing in the whole history of the electoral college. As a result the Emperor was requested to summon Luther to Worms. Popular feeling was too strong for his Holiness's representative to be given satisfaction. But there would be no discussion with the heretic who had already been condemned by the Pope, and he would be asked if he was ready to retract on the points listed in the bull. His attacks on papal authority and canon law would be examined later on: the Diet itself should discuss the grievances of the German nation against the Roman Curia.

Aleander was desperate: 'No one knows any longer what should be done or how to proceed. What will happen if Martin comes? We must fear the worst.' The situation was so much the more uncomfortable as the policy of the Curia in Italy and Spain made the Emperor and his ministers disinclined to act. Gattinara went so far as to say one day: 'Make sure your Pope does not play a trick on us. He will get what he wants from us. But if he does anything nasty, just see what a mess we will land you in!'

In a book which arrived at Worms just then, Luther defended

the theses condemned by Leo X's first bull. He justified his attitude in these terms:

'Many ask why I think I have the right to teach everyone. I reply that: First, it is not I who have put myself forward. Personally, I would prefer to retire to my corner. But my enemies always make me come out by trickery or by threats. They use me to draw attention to themselves; and when their stratagem miscarries, they accuse me of pride.

'Secondly, supposing I had appointed myself master of the truth why should that not have come from God? The Scripture shows that there is always only one prophet at a time, chosen usually from men of low status. In every age, the saints have preached against the authorities—kings, princes, doctors, priests—and have risked their heads.

'I do not say that I am a prophet. But the more I am scorned, the more they assert that they are right, the more I must anxiously wonder if I am not perhaps under God's orders. The Lord is wondrous in his works and his judgements. Power does not impress him. If I am not a prophet, I am at least sure that the Word of God is on my side and not on theirs. . . . For I have the Scripture on my side, while they have only their own doctrine. This encourages me to fear them less the more they scorn and persecute me. There were many asses in Balaam's time; yet God chose to speak through none except Balaam's ass.

'I am accused of preaching a new doctrine. That is untrue! I only say that those who are responsible for maintaining true Christianity, that is to say the bishops and theologians, have let it completely disappear.

'I have no doubt that in all ages revealed truth has lived on in some hearts, even if only in those of babes in arms. I do not reject the Fathers of the Church. But like all men, they sometimes make mistakes. I believe them only to the extent that their assertions can be proved by Scripture. Only Scripture has never erred.

'That so many men are against me, just because I rely solely on Scripture, does not make me fearful. On the contrary, such persecution is a strength and consolation. Invariably in the Bible the persecutors are wrong and the persecuted are right. It warns us all the time that the majority is always on the side of falsehood, and the solitary ones alone know the truth.

'As for the troubles which led me to my present attitude, they necessarily accompany truth. The evil teachers, on the other hand, always have order on their side.'

Whichever way he turned, Aleander could see no way out. He watched powerless as the Diet firmly rejected his plan for an edict. On 6 March, the Emperor ordered the drafting of the act of convocation and safe-conduct for Luther. The nuncio fought a rearguard action without much hope to prevent the excommunicated heretic from being treated with too much respect.

But the real question had to do with the Pope. The German nation yearns for physical contact with its heroes; the Italians do not understand this visceral and illogical desire. The wish of the majority to remain faithful to Rome, their sincere respect for the rights of the Pope as supreme judge, excommunication which prevented any contact with the intangible world, the interdict which in theory required the suspension of the sacrament at Worms as long as Luther stayed there, all this achieved nothing. Luther's magnetism was too strong, stronger than any reason. Second thoughts would come only later.

Aleander had to do some explaining to Rome about the terms under which the safe-conduct was drawn up: 'Honourable, dear and pious Martin, we and the States of the Holy Roman Empire presently assembled have resolved and desired to hear you on the doctrines and books put forth by you over a period of time. We summon you to come here and we grant you in our name and the name of the Empire every security and guarantee as the safe-conduct here enclosed attests. With the wish that you respond to our order and do not neglect to appear before us, that you present yourself here without fail within the twenty-one days provided by the terms of our safe-conduct, and that no one cause you evil or violence . . .'

Having failed to prevent the excommunicate being summoned, Aleander tried pressure. He got the Emperor to order the seizure of Luther's books and with immediate effect. He knew that in the Elector of Saxony's view the desirability of Luther's coming to Worms was questionable: if the heretic should become disheartened or lay the blame on the Emperor, the papal party would regain the initiative.

But if the nuncio was not far from the truth in thinking that he could still intimidate the Saxons at Worms, he had, as ever, not really understood Luther. Luther was not one of those humanists whom the study of the past had made timid. In a way—no one could explain why—he was free of the burden of the old world and rushing at full speed towards the future. On 16 April, late in the morning, Aleander was informed:

'Luther has arrived.'

Rome had lost another round.

20

Charles The Fifth

Spalatin had installed Luther near the Swan Inn, where the Elector was staying, in a room rented from the knights of Malta.

The infidel had made a triumphal progress across Germany. An imperial herald in livery led the way and drew attention to the canopied cart lent by the Wittenberg Town Council. More than a hundred armed men accompanied the mysterious monk in his habit, who excited in turn enthusiasm and uproar as he passed. He had been told to be suspicious of poison and in fact had once been very sick. But for the time being he was tired out, overwhelmed and pampered. Everyone wanted to see the arch-heretic. One priest embraced him as if he were a relic.

In the midst of this crowd he was, as always, alone. The Elector made no secret of the fact that he could do nothing for him. At Oppenheim, the last stop before Worms, he had refused an invitation to take refuge in the Ebernburg under the protection of Sickingen's soldiers. Father Glapion proposed to go there to meet him; Luther, however, indicated to the imperial confessor that he would willingly receive him, but at Worms. His instinct told him that whatever happened, he could rely only on himself. He was not mistaken: Hutten had been bribed and now served under Charles the Fifth.

Luther did not know what would happen at Worms. The texts received from the Emperor were very vague and he only deducted from them that he was not being asked in advance to retract. Having therefore nothing to prepare for, he yielded to curiosity and to the visitor's questions.

The uncertainty about the procedure to be adopted remained

up to the last moment, because the nuncios who had always opposed Luther's presence at Worms and the statesmen both strove to influence the outcome. The Emperor was perhaps the only one to see clearly what he wanted. The decision to ask Luther simply whether or not he retracted his books was undoubtedly due to him. The pressure of opinion dictated that the 'examination' should take place before the Diet. Luther was summoned to appear on the afternoon of 17 April at 4 o'clock. But at 2 o'clock it was still undecided who would put the fateful question to him. The choice fell in the end on the leading official of the Archbishop-Elector of Trier. Ever since the agreement made at the beginning of 1519 between Miltitz and the Prince of Saxony, this magistrate, Von Eck, had been destined in any case to interrogate Luther.

When the marshal, von Pappenheim, brought the order to present himself before the Diet, Luther had just returned from giving the last sacraments to a dying man. He trimmed his tonsure, leaving only the crown of hair which the rule prescribed. The Saxon court had advised him to take care of his appearance, his manners and his language.

They came for him at 4 o'clock. The crowd was so thick that he had to make his way through the gardens; probably only those who had ensconced themselves on the rooftops could see him. The soldiers had some difficulty maintaining a semblance of order. He was brought through a side door into the room where the Diet was assembled, and hundreds of glances fell on him. The whole of Germany was there: the six electoral princes (only the King of Bohemia was absent), the Archduke Ferdinand, the Emperor's brother, two landgraves, five margraves, twenty-seven dukes, numerous counts and prelates, counsellors, lawyers and some guards; and, on a canopied seat, the Emperor.

Apart from some privileged persons who had reserved places or who had been able to install themselves on stone seats along the walls, everyone was standing and squashing each other in order the better to see and hear.

Only Aleander was missing. The dignity of the Holy See forbade him from endorsing with his presence the illegal examination of an excommunicate before a lay tribunal. But he kept himself informed minute by minute of the progress of the meeting.

Luther and the officers accompanying him with difficulty made their way through to the Emperor. Here the two champions faced each other in a battle of a new kind: the master of half the world confronted the leader of the great majority of Germans. For, like Glapion, many were still charmed by Luther's first writings. Of the two, he was the emperor of Germany, and Charles knew it. With one gesture, Luther could unleash a revolt which would finish off the Emperor. But the little Burgundian had resolved 'That man is not going to make a heretic of me.'

Luther noticed a friendly face: Peutinger, his host at Augsburg. 'So you are here, doctor!'

Von Pappenheim called him to order:

'You must not open your mouth until you are invited to do so.'

He was not forbidden, however, to open his eyes. He looked all around him, up towards the roof, down to his feet, and examined faces in the crowd, without being disturbed by the Emperor's presence. His black penetrating eyes made more than one person ill at ease.

On a bench was the evidence in question: about thirty books, piled up—*his* books.

Von Eck began to speak.

'Martin Luther! His Imperial Majesty has caused you to appear to put two questions to you: Do you recognise these books published under your name as yours? Are you prepared to disavow them, as a whole or in part?'

Before Luther could reply, the Saxon counsellor, Schurf, asked that the titles of the books be read. Luther, for his part, was astonished that such a collection should have been brought together. Perhaps he had forgotten the nuncio's profession?

With a measured voice, but with impressive gestures, Luther declared first in German and then in Latin:

'These are indeed my books. As for the second question, a momentous one for faith, for the salvation of souls and our highest good here below, that is to say the Word of God, I ask for a delay before replying.'

The audience was all ears. The Emperor had not understood. Luther's reply had to be translated into French.

This reply had caught the judges napping. They quickly conferred. Was the heretic going to play games again? To guard against this threat it was decided to give him only twenty-four hours for reflection, and to insist on an oral reply without any written defence. Von Eck thought it expedient to direct a further word at Luther.

'The summons must have made it clear that you came here only to retract.'

No, Luther had not understood that, for the very good reason that no one had said any such thing to him. But he did not have the opportunity to reply. At a signal from the Emperor, he was led out.

That evening, he sent a note to a friend: 'I appeared today before the Emperor and was asked if I wished to disavow my books. I said that I would reply tomorrow. I will not retract one iota. May Christ help me!'

Despite the prohibition, he prepared his reply in writing.

On the 18th, the crowd was even thicker than on the previous day, even though a larger room had been chosen. Some were there from ten in the morning. The imperial throne could not be made ready until near 6 o'clock and as his Majesty and their Highnesses appeared, night was falling. Torches were lit.

It was only with difficulty that Luther could find a place! Mingling with princes, who were also obliged to stand up, he listened to Von Eck's questions, the same ones as the day before. He then began to speak in German in a clear and confident voice.

'I appeared in all obedience at the hour appointed yesterday evening.

'I beg your most serene Majesty, as well as your distinguished lordships, to listen carefully to my case. It is, I dare to believe, that of justice and truth. . . . The only evidence I can give is that, right up until this day, my sole concern has been the glory of God and the instruction of the faithful in pure truth.

'I have been asked whether I recognise as mine the books gathered together here. My reply is yes, as long as my enemies have changed nothing in them. I deny any interpretation.

'I have also been asked if I intend to defend these books, or rather if I intend to retract them. I reply on this matter that my books are of three kinds:

'The first kind deal with faith and morals, in a way that has never provoked objection. My opponents themselves recognise their usefulness for Christian people. The bull considered them inoffensive; but that did not prevent it from condemning them. If I retracted them, I would be the only one against them. I do not retract them.

'The second category makes a case against the papacy because it tortures consciences and squanders our people's resources. To retract these books would be to consent to this tyranny and approve its continuation. The people's predicament would be even more intolerable, especially because it could be asserted that I have done nothing but obey the orders of your Majesty and the whole Empire.

'The third category is directed against private persons who defended the Roman tyranny and wished to overturn what I was teaching about faith. I ought to have been less brutal towards them, especially in matters touching religion. But I do not pretend to be a saint. Besides, the debate is not on the perfection of the Christian life, but on the truth of what is taught about Jesus Christ.

'It is thus impossible for me to retract these various writings. But I am only a man, and I cannot defend myself otherwise than did Christ himself before Annas. A servant had slapped him and he asked simply: "If I have spoken evil, show me what I have said which is wrong."

'The Lord, who was incapable of error, has allowed his teaching to be debated. All the more reason for me, the scum of the earth, a man always open to error, to desire and expect my teaching to be debated in the same way. I therefore beg your Majesty, your distinguished lordships and whoever else can, from the greatest to the smallest, to debate, to convince me of my errors, to refute me by the writings of the prophets and the Gospel.

'If I could thus be better instructed, none would be more eager than I to retract whatever errors there are. I would be the first to throw my books on the fire.

'What I have just said shows that I have carefully considered everything: the crises, dangers, agonies and dissensions which may loom up in the world because of my teaching, and about which I have already been warned in no uncertain terms.

'However, it pleases me to see passions and dissension arising about the Word of God, for is it not said that on earth: "I have come not to bring peace but the sword; I have come to make division between a man and his father . . ."?

'Let us remember that our God is wondrous and terrible in his judgements. To reject the Word of God for the sake of peace and quiet would be a terrible beginning to this imperial reign. Scripture shows continually that God surprises the experts in their cleverness and overturns the mountains before they are aware of it. It is God who must be feared before all else.

'I say all this without thinking that such an assembly as this need my teaching or my warnings. But I have no right to conceal from Germany the duty I owe her.

'With these words, I commend myself to your Majesty and your lordships, humbly beseeching you not to allow the anger of my opponents to discredit me unjustly.

'I have spoken.

'Do you wish me to repeat it in Latin?'

Luther began to feel hot in this packed room, where he was hemmed in on all sides. When he started to repeat his declaration in the language of the learned, those who had understood the German asked themselves: Is it Yes, or No?

The princes withdrew to get to the bottom of the matter. The man had said that he was ready to be taught a better doctrine by someone, however lowly, capable of interpreting Scripture. What could one think of such a request? The prince-bishops thought that, since the Church had defined doctrines clearly enough, there was no point in trying to say them better, or in saying anything else. But the examination could not be allowed to fizzle out. There must be a conclusion; Luther must be obliged to say whether or not he retracted. Accordingly, Eck was asked to bring the matter to an end.

The meeting resumed. Eck launched into an interminable discourse aimed at undermining Luther's morale. He reproached him for having evaded the essential question and explained that no one would discuss points of doctrine long since fixed by councils and that Luther had only to believe like everyone else. When he felt the ground was adequately prepared, he shot out point blank the deciding question:

'Reply honestly and sincerely, without evasion: do you wish to retract your books and all the errors which they contain. Yes or No?'

'Your most serene Majesty and your lordships demand a simple reply. I am going to give it to you straight from the horse's mouth, without beating about the bush:

'Here it is: unless I am convinced by the evidence of Scripture or by plain reason—for I accept neither the Pope nor the councils by themselves, since it is clear that they have often been mistaken and contradictory—I am bound by the Scriptural texts I have quoted and my conscience belongs to the Word of God. I cannot and will not retract anything, for to act against one's conscience is neither safe nor honest'.

So strong were his feelings that Luther suddenly abandoned Latin to cry out in his mother tongue:

'I cannot. Do with me what you will. God help me!'

This time everyone understood. Some princes began to move towards the door. Eck tried to grasp the bomb before it exploded:

'Forget your conscience, unhappy man! It is deceived. You could never prove that the councils have been mistaken in matters of faith. At the most in matters of discipline . . .'

'I can prove what I put forward . . .'

The Emperor made a signal. Two guards hurried Luther away. The crowd let out a roar.

'Don't worry,' cried Luther, 'these are my guardian angels!'

The mob crowded behind the trio, waving their arms as a sign of victory. The Spanish guards shouted as the heretic passed by:

'*Al fuego! Al fuego!*'

The Germans did not understand enough Spanish to unsheath their swords.

Having returned safe and sound to his lodgings, Luther in turn raised his arms to heaven:

'It's all right now! All right!'

He was content because the conviction for which he had sacrificed everything had not let him down at the most crucial moment of his career. It had enabled him to say what was necessary. In everything that he had said, in a gathering which had impressed him more than he cared to admit, there had not been a word too much, not a word out of place. It had contained the whole Luther case in a nutshell.

Supposing that he had been able to retract, the gathering would certainly have ended up as a general massacre. The tension which had been built up for over three years in so many hearts and lives would have been shown to be a hideous farce. The *yes* as well as the *no* of this man, at this point in history, contained an explosive power which was scarcely tolerable. The wonder was not his obstinacy, nor his persistence, but that, without having sought it, he had from the very beginning put his finger on a linchpin of Christianity, of the human spirit and of history.

Yes, he was a prisoner—as so many other prophets before him. Prisoner of a message which had taken him by surprise. His deep-seated honesty could do nothing but obey the iron law of his faith. But it was not the faith of the Church.

On the 19th, young Charles called together the electors and the other princes. Aleander was also there.

'I have called you together so that you can offer me your advice. What do we decide about this Brother Martin?'

There was a discussion. A delay was requested to give time for reflection.

'Very well. But I am first going to indicate to you my personal position.'

And, before his speechless audience, the following text, which the master of the Holy Roman Empire had written with his own hand, was read out in French:

'As you know, I number among my ancestors the most Christian emperors of the noble German nation, the Catholic kings of Spain, the archdukes of Austria and the dukes of Burgundy. All of them remained until their death loyal sons of the Roman Church, defenders of the Catholic faith, of its customs, its laws and its form of worship. They passed on this heritage to me and up till now I have always followed their example.

'I am resolved to abide by all that has been done since the Council of Constance. This solitary brother surely is mistaken when he sets himself against the views of all Christendom. Otherwise, Christendom would have been in error for more than a thousand years.

'I have therefore decided to pledge to this cause my kingdoms and possessions, my friends, my body and my blood, my life and my soul. It would be shameful for us and for you, members of the noble German nation, if today, by our negligence, the least suspicion of heresy and debasement of religion should enter into men's hearts.

'We have heard Luther's discourse here, and I tell you that I regret having delayed so long in taking measures against him. I have no wish ever to hear him again.

'He has his safe-conduct, but I consider him henceforth as a notorious heretic and I expect you as true Christians to do the same.'

A shiver went through the audience. Their faces were as pale as shrouds. Heresy was proclaimed by the supreme law-giver of the Empire—and there was only one sentence: the stake.

All present, or nearly all, were implicated.

The inexperienced monarch had decided. He had refused to play along with those who offered Luther to him as an effective means of bringing pressure to bear on the Pope. A Charles the Fifth did not eat that particular bread. He did not yet know that one day he would sack Rome with his troops—Spanish Catholics and Lutheran footsoldiers. But he knew that the Empire had no other master than he and no other faith than his. Luther might rule the roost in Saxony, the Emperor would let him have the electors, the princes, the landgraves, the kings, everything—except the Catholic faith. Luther had found the only challenger worthy of debating with him, but they were never to see each other again.

21
The Death-throes of Unity

The Emperor's verdict had not only upset the princes, but the whole town was beside itself. Desperate plans were made to save Luther. That very evening, groups of people consulted together. . . .

The following morning, inscriptions and tracts were found all over Worms. Luther was taken to task: 'Let the Pope damn you. Let the Emperor damn you! Frederick also will condemn you and will clearly not respect the safe-conduct. Poor fool Luther! You only rehash old errors, you have said nothing new.' But disturbing statements were also to be found, such as the one at the town hall: 'We are 400 conspirators from the nobility. We are declaring war on the princes of the Diet and especially on the Archbishop of Mainz. I don't write very well but I intend to cause great havoc. I have 8,000 men. Bundschuh! Bundschuh! Bundschuh!' On the town gates, an unknown hand had drawn this simple phrase: 'Unhappy the people whose king is a child!'

There was much commotion. Was the boiler going to burst? The Archbishop of Mainz urgently sent his brother, the Elector of Brandenburg, to the Emperor to suggest that his Majesty should agree to have Luther questioned once more by some doctors in the presence of a few princes.

Charles refused categorically. The nuncio had warned him about Albert of Mainz's double game. But the Lutheran party, which had its conspirators and hired assassins, laid down the law at the Diet.

The Diet supported Albert's request. Luther should be confronted with three or four honourable persons who were experts in Holy Scripture, and whose task would be to show his errors and seek to refute them. It must not be possible to say that his theses had not even been discussed: the people could conclude that he had been condemned without having been cross-examined.

On the 22nd, the Emperor yielded to the pressure. He held to his position, but agreed to three days' delay. If the Diet wished to try to obtain Luther's retraction, they were free to do do. As for his Imperial Majesty, he did not want to be implicated or represented in it.

The Diet, which deliberated that very day on the *Grievances of the German nation*, named a commission made up of the two Electors of Brandenburg and Trier, Duke George of Saxony, the Bishops of Augsburg and Brandenburg, Peutinger and two other persons, one of whom was Bock, a representative of Strasbourg. Only Bock and Peutinger were not declared enemies of Luther.

The examination was led by Jerome Vehus, Chancellor of the State of Baden. It was friendly in tone and Luther had the impression that they wanted to induce him to give up his appeal to the Bible. He could only repeat that he would yield only to better reasons or to a better interpretation of Scripture.

The Archbishop of Trier then tried another approach. He invited Luther to talk with him alone, each to be assisted by two experts. Luther came with Schurf and Amsdorf, and the Archbishop chose Von Eck and a man who had never seen Luther before, the Canon Cochlaeus, a humanist, dean of the Frankfurt Collegiate Church.

No sooner had the colloquy begun that it was interrupted: the Archbishop's presence was requested. Cochlaeus took advantage of the situation to put in a word:

'If you continue like this, you are going to drag down to ruin with you the brilliant Philip Melanchthon and many other young men from whom we are expecting a renewal of thought.'

'What can I do?'

'Change your mind!'

The Prince-Bishop returned and they took their seats. Von Eck pressed Luther not to be obstinate in his interpretation of the Scripture, against the whole Church. This sort of obstinacy was found in all heretics. But Luther claimed the right to contradict the decrees of the councils. As the Apostle said: 'If something is revealed to one of the hearers, let him who speaks be silent.' This elicited the rejoinder that it was possible to contradict during the discussion, but not once a common decision had been taken.

The discussion was getting bogged down. Cochlaeus, who wanted to get it moving again, took up Luther's previous statement that he did not claim to have received revelation.

'So, you are inspired.'

'Me? . . . Yes!'

'But you have just said the opposite!'

'Not at all!'

'What do you base it on? Where are your miracles? What sign do you give? Everyone can say as much . . .'

The interview began turning to Luther's disadvantage. The Archbishop put an end to it by declaring that it was time for lunch.

Cochlaeus pressed his point further.

'You have rejected so many things which good people consider worthy of belief: why not reject your own ideas in which no one believes?'

'I have not written, in any case, against private individuals.'

'And Leo X, whom you regard as a heretic, apostate, infidel and tyrant?'

'Leo X is a public person.'

Luther took his leave. The canon found that a stubborn man has an answer to everything.

Stubborn? . . . What if this were not the case? Had not Luther begun by asking: 'What shall I do?' . . . Like so many others before him, Cochlaeus gradually came to consider that he had perhaps found the way to deal with Luther. He would seek him out where he was staying with his followers. In this familiar environment, in confidence, Luther would be more relaxed.

After lunch, without telling anyone of his plan, the canon went to the house of the knights of Malta. In the boiler-room he found a group of people who invited him to sit down. Amsdorf, appropriately, was there. He sat beside him and remarked very audibly that peace was better than obstinacy. But an Augustinian friar, in a habit like Luther's, goaded him in a scornful tone to debate on this subject with him. The worthy canon, disconcerted, replied that he was talking to Amsdorf. And, stung into action, he went on:

'Do you believe, worthy friar, that no men worthy of this name are to be found outside your hole of Wittenberg? What had the Dominican prior done to you the day you grabbed him as he was coming down from the pulpit and dragged him in front of the congregation, under the pretext that he had badly interpreted Saint Paul? What actions would they not risk to cancel Father Luther's safe-conduct?'

The canon seemed to have made his point. 'Take no notice! The friar wants to be more knowledgeable than all of us especially when he has had a drink.'

Laughter broke out and the aggressor beat a retreat. Luther sat down phlegmatically beside the canon and the conversation continued. Cochlaeus pressed him again to make peace with the Church. How would he and his partisans succeed with the Pope, the Emperor, the princes and the Estates of the Holy Roman Empire united against him?

'I didn't know,' said Luther, 'that the Emperor agreed with the princes in declaring me a heretic if I did not retract.'

'You cannot cope with everyone. If you don't give in for your own sake, do so at least for the people and the youth. . . .'

The young people who were there protested. This canon got on their nerves. One of them asked:

'Why do you lay the blame on learning, when you yourself were a humanist?'

'I continue to love studying, but the Catholic faith comes first.'

To raise the level of the conversation, the jurist Schurf invited Cochlaeus, who had written a book against Luther, to name at least one of the latter's errors.

'To be frank, I have not read most of his works, since I attached little importance to them until I came across the *Babylonian Captivity*. And even this book I have read only in part. But what I have read of it has offended me in the extreme. . . .'

So this was the 'expert' chosen by the Archbishop of Trier to be on a small committee which had to cope with a crisis as big as Germany and Christendom! This was the inspired man who considered himself called to act as conciliator: it was worth ten florins to him from Aleander and a free dispensation from Caracciolo. . . . But it was difficult to see how he was going to earn his salary.

Alone against all these Lutherans and Luther in person, not having read very much of Luther, but called upon to show at least one error made by the man whom he attacked with all the pride of his orthodoxy, he had to state precisely where he saw heresy arise.

'Why make such a fuss so that people can communicate in both kinds? You admit yourself that it is not indispensable for a layman to communicate in bread and wine.'

'Matthew said: "Drink, all of you".'

'But those who receive only the bread drink . . . under the element of bread, for the whole Christ is contained in the bread!'

'Why not give the laity the complete sacrament?'

'But it is complete! The whole Christ is contained in the bread as in the wine; in the bread and wine . . .'

'Christ instituted this sacrament in two kinds, the bread and the wine.'

'He also instituted it after supper, but that doesn't oblige us to communicate after supper.'

'The sacrament is clearer when its two elements are brought together.'

'I know, but it is more risky. For to give the chalice to people of little learning easily leads to a loss of respect. The Church had very important reasons for distributing the sacrament only under the element of bread . . .'

Cochlaeus defended himself well, like Eck before him. They were playing at disputation which attracted the amateurs. The boiler-room filled up with more and more Lutherans.

Provoked again, the canon attacked on the subject of transubstantiation. . . . He rested his case on the Lateran Council of 1215, which amused everyone. How could anyone still cite the councils? The man was taken less and less seriously. At one moment Luther even begged him not to use bad grammar. The words *corpitas*, *panitas* were heard. . . .

The honour of the Frankfurt chapter had to be saved. Cochlaeus suddenly challenged Luther:

'I am ready to dispute on equal terms with you. But you must first give up your safe-conduct. Whoever loses will be burnt at the stake!'

Luther stopped laughing—understandably! Everyone asked in German why Luther should renounce his safe-conduct.

'If he takes no risks, why should I?'

Cochlaeus's strange proposal came out of a conversation he had had some days earlier with two lawyers: one of them had asked where were the theologians who claimed to be able to refute Luther. Why weren't they coming forward to dispute? Luther, he added, was ready to denounce his safe-conduct and all his privileges in order to be able to discuss his doctrine.

'But for such a dispute, judges would be needed.'

'What judges?' cried the Lutherans, 'the Pope's?'

'No, judges named by the Emperor and the Diet.'

'Well, as for me,' Luther said, 'I choose as a judge a child of eight or nine years.'

'Really? What a fine judge! But, no more jokes. Luther, I have not come to take up cudgels with you. I have something to say to you which I cannot say here.'

'If you want to talk, then,' intervened the count of Mansfeld, 'go up to Luther's room.'

So now the canon and the heretic were alone together, or almost alone. A friar was sharing his room, partly because of lack of space, partly as a security measure, and Luther did not want him to leave. Cochlaeus had insisted that there would be no witnesses to the interview, and almost went to the point of unbuttoning his gown to prove that he was not armed. Finally, not wanting to be at a disadvantage, he got his nephew to come up.

The conversation started off easily. Luther calmly recounted his impressions of the days which he had just lived through. He admitted that he had overstepped the mark a little with respect to the Pope, but he had at least achieved one result: no one was any longer talking of indulgences.

'The apostolic nuncio,' Cochlaeus began, 'has given me to understand today that you are only being asked to revoke those of your writings which are openly against the faith of the Catholic Church. For the rest, the Emperor and the princes can name some learned men to read your works and separate the good grain from the chaff. What is good will be kept and what is bad will be destroyed.

'If fear or shame prevent you from returning to Wittenberg, the Emperor and the Archbishop of Trier will provide you with the means of living elsewhere peacefully and honestly. Since you are young and strong, of exceptional intelligence, an unremitting worker, of unusual erudition and universal renown, you can be most useful by dedicating yourself to the pious and peaceable interpretation of Scripture. You can restore the peace that you have subverted to the people of God. All that is needed is for you to retract. If you don't want to do it for yourself, at least have pity on Philip Melanchthon . . .'

This name stirred Luther. The two speakers wept copiously. Cochlaeus again spoke of the clemency of the Pope, who had forgiven so much. . . . As for indulgences, far from being abolished, the canon predicted for them a great future in the Church.

It was time to finish.

'My dear doctor,' Luther said, 'there are so many people more powerful and more intelligent than I who have the same ideas that my retraction in itself would change nothing. That is all I can say.'

The two men shook hands in tears, each one vowing to bring the other low by their writing throughout the lives. . . . They were destined to keep their word.

This tragi-comedy unfolded while the Diet's commission was making its report. The Emperor's entourage, in the name of his Majesty, urged Luther's immediate departure. The Elector of Trier, doubtless out of regard for his friend Frederick, wanted to try a new initiative. Aleander, who mistrusted this, insisted that there should be no infringements of papal prerogatives.

So on the afternoon of the 25th, Luther returned to the Elector of Trier. The latter offered to protect him: he would recommend him to a good priory under the protection of a powerful castle. He would be admitted to the Bishop's table and invited to advise him. Luther declined.

The Archbishop then offered him the following choices: 1. Submit the affair to the joint judgement of the Pope and Emperor; 2. to the Emperor alone, who would settle things with the Pope; or 3. refer it to the Emperor and the Diet; or 4. retract the most glaring errors and submit the others to a future Council.

Luther did not even stop to study these splendid possibilities. He refused point-blank, at least having the moral satisfaction of establishing that, to make him retract, his opponents were ready to deny the principles in the name of which they were hounding him. For the Archbishop's plan was the complete renunciation of papal primacy. Why, there was little point in regretting that one had fallen out with everybody.

Empty-handed again, the Elector threw in the sponge. The Emperor, who was apprised of the situation that evening, sent his secretary with the Trier official, the chancellor of Austria and two witnesses to give Luther notice to leave the next day,

26 April. The safe-conduct would protect him for another twenty-one days. He must not preach nor meet the people nor publish anything during his journey. He should wait at Wittenberg for the decision which would be made about him.

The luggage was soon ready. Luther would at least carry off his head! Before settling down in the Wittenberg Council's uncomfortable cart for the long days ahead, he toasted plenty of bread for himself and downed some large bumpers of wine. Aleander was scandalised.

When he had passed through the city gates, surrounded by a cluster of Wittenbergers on horseback, lethargy returned to the little Rhine city. But there was one lasting souvenir of these events of the month of April: the Edict of Worms. Aleander, in fact, encountered no more resistance. He attained his goal, or at least he thought he had.

For while the text which would make it possible for Luther to be seized was being prepared, unbelievable news spread through the whole of Germany: Luther had disappeared!

The most contradictory news passed from mouth to mouth: the monk had been butchered, his corpse had been found in a mineshaft. . . . The painter Albrecht Dürer expressed his sorrow in his diary. His dream of one day painting the portrait of the man he regarded as a martyr would not be realised.

Those in the know watched the Elector of Saxony. He had declared at the Diet, on 12 May, that he did not know where Luther was. . . .

22
The Outlaw

A little secondary road, four days walk from Wittenberg. Whichever way one turned, only Luthers were to be seen! Having left most of his companions on the highway which led to Gotha, Martin Luther, followed by Amsdorf and the friar who had picked a quarrel with Cochlaeus, had made a detour in the direction of Möhra, to see his uncle Heinrich. The Luther-clan had welcomed him with open arms and he had spent the night in his ancestral home. In the morning, he preached to the peasants in the open air. The village had no church and perhaps it was better this way. For at Eisenach, on 1 May, the priest had not let him mount the pulpit before having made clear that he himself had nothing to do with it.

The Luthers were not afraid of the curse which an excommunicate left in his wake. They had ridden out to hearten him on his way, but as the afternoon wore on they had to part company. While the family returned to its fields, the cart carrying Doctor Luther and his friends plunged into the shadows of a wood.

Since the departure from Worms, everything had been peaceful, and they had been able to send back the imperial herald, whose protection no longer seemed necessary.

At Friedberg, the Mountain of Peace, some distance beyond Frankfurt, Luther had written to his most Serene Majesty Charles the Fifth, Emperor-elect of the Romans, King of Spain, of the two Sicilies and Jerusalem, Archduke of Austria, and Duke of Burgundy. To make matters clear, he was determined to state precisely why, since all his books were founded on the clear texts of Scripture, it had not appeared either possible or proper for him to deny the Word of God. His dearest desire would be that his Majesty should himself examine the writings or have them examined by someone who was capable of judging them, from the point of view of the prophets and the Gospel. . . .

During the prolonged resistance to the theses which, in his naivety, Luther had thought he should offer for the Church's consideration, his conscience had struggled with an insoluble inconsistency. What he found in Scripture seemed right to him. Otherwise, he would not have wearied the world with his claims. On the other hand, it was clear that the official authority of the Church did not see in Scripture what he saw. He could therefore not exclude the possibility that there was an interpretation other than his and truer than his.

But Scripture could not be taken lightly. To ask him to retract his scriptural theses without offering him in return the true interpretation of the Word of God was to invite him to close up the Bible for good. He had asked the Church to help him move forward in his knowledge of Scripture and the answer had been that he must stop trying to understand it. The papal Church drew from its resources a truth designed to provide for men's day-to-day needs, needs which were not always very great, as the success of the indulgences had shown. Since this suited the people, they had been given indulgences galore. In the same way, Luther had tried to spread abroad the mystery of the Word of God, taken directly from Scripture. He had no less success. It had been instantaneous, like something so obvious that no one had ever given it a thought.

He had been reproached most vigorously for not having taken anything from the councils, the papal texts, Church law or theologians' studies. He had indeed attacked all that, and often clumsily. But the worst thing was that he had no need to do so. The layers added by each generation to the doctrinal edifice seemed less solid than the foundations. He would be willing to give up all the branches of the tree to see it start off again from its roots.

Why did none of those who were made his judges want to wet even a little finger in this interminable debate which, from the first thunderclap, had destroyed the unexceptional life of which Luther, the miner's son, had dreamed as much as his father? Were they afraid of being caught in the mesh in which he himself had been the prey? Was Scripture a burning bush which man should not approach without the risk of taking the path of the Exodus? Having brought the Christian into contact with the mysterious, was the Church then incapable of following him in his desperate search for ever-vanishing horizons? Was it necessary, by discipline and social conformity, to pass over in silence what was perceived only in the form of words? In a sense, Luther thought of himself as victim of an unjust destiny, victim of the contradictions of Christianity. But what of the others: Leo X, Cajetan, Eck, Charles V . . . ?

Would the imperial heir of so many Catholic ancestors understand that this was something to do with the Church rather than with Luther? One could proscribe and kill the heretic, but one could not stifle the questions which his conscience brought to light for an institution which God instructs through the living as well as the dead.

After the letter to the Emperor, a word must be sent to the Diet, which was in the process of hammering out its edict. Luther was satisfied to repeat the same thing.

His friend Cranach, the Wittenberg painter, had as much right to a message, which he sent from Frankfurt:

'You want to know what happened at Worms: Here it is:

' "These books are yours?"

' "Yes."

' "Do you want to retract what they contain?"

"No."

' "Be off with you!" '

Amsdorf cried out:

'Look! There! . . .'

Four men on horseback barred the way. Luther grasped his Hebrew Bible and his Greek New Testament. The friar leapt like a hare into the nearest thicket. There was only time to catch a glimpse of the bottom of his breeches in the arc traced by his robe.

Threatened by crossbows, the cart was brought to a stop.

'Doctor Luther?'

'That's me.'

Amsdorf let fly with the most forceful verbal barrage allowed by good manners; but he learned more in a few moments than in his whole life. Crying out louder than he, the others snatched the heretic and tied his hands. The compromising books were thrown into a beggar's sack. A brief command and the horsemen disappeared around a bend, dragging on a leash the doctor who was out of breath keeping up with the horses.

Well done! Amsdorf could let Spalatin know that everything had gone well. Only the friar was annoyed. He was not in the know.

Scarcely were they out of sight than Luther was given a horse. A gallop, to get rid of possible pursuers, then a long walk along little paths and fallow lands, where they could be sure of not meeting anyone.

Night had long fallen when, after an interminable ride, the little band suddenly found itself before a draw-bridge. The visitors must have been expected for the heavy door opened immediately. Behind them the drawbridge raised itself with its grinding mechanism. Safe at last!

In the dimly-lit courtyard, two men welcomed the travellers who dismounted one after the other.

'Sternberg!'

'Captain Von Berlepsch!'

They sounded friendly. Without losing a moment, Luther was led to a little two-roomed suite.

'You must get rid of this cassock immediately. Here are the clothes for you to wear. You are absolutely forbidden to go out of here before your tonsure has disappeared. You must also grow a moustache and beard. Junker George, I wish you good night!'

'Junker George' made sure that his Bible and his New Testament had been brought along. He had his plan. This fortress, whose thick walls held a sepulchral cold which resisted all fires, would give the German people at the same time its common bond and its tongue. Throughout endless lonely days, enlivened only by the servants who brought his meals twice a day, the outlaw piled up the pages of his translation of the Bible, shot through with the music of the birds and woven with a kind of language which had never before seen the light of day.

The Holy Roman Empire did not forget him. Some weeks after his disappearance, he was brought a copy of the Edict of Worms, dated 8 May 1521, signed in fact on the 26th, Trinity Sunday. He was nothing but an outlaw.

Aleander had lost sleep over this document—his guiding hand could be felt throughout it. Its substance was as follows:

'Friar Martin Luther, of the order of the Augustinians, has propagated through his writings errors ancient and modern, has attacked the number, the order and the use of the sacraments, disparaged the Holy Laws of marriage, outraged and vilified the Pope, poured scorn on the priesthood, denied free will and set the faithful free of all morality and all law; he has burned books of canon law, blasphemed the Councils, in particular that of Constance, and his word is destructive of all true faith and all good order.

'Scornful of the forbearance exercised towards him and of all warnings given him, he has held obstinately to his errors, and must therefore be regarded as a declared heretic: he and his abettors and partisans have been put under the Ban of the Empire; no one can receive or defend him, everyone is bound to arrest him and deliver him to the Emperor; his books as well as the pamphlets, lampoons and caricatures against the Pope, the prelates and the Catholic faith, must be destroyed and burnt; booksellers who do not comply will be punished with severe penalties. For the future, to prevent the distribution of such writings, all books dealing with religion must be submitted before printing for the approval of the ordinary of the locality and of the faculty of theology of the nearest university.'

Rome could not wait to see the heretic at the stake. It had

made a down-payment. A wood and cardboard Luther had been made, as for the carnival, and had been attached to a stake. At his feet, his books in which no one was interested. Cochlaeus had already shown that it was not necessary to read them in order to refute them. The Roman crowds lavishly applauded the bonfire of the Gospel of saving faith. The faith was preserved.

There was, moreover, some point in keeping the fire burning. for here from the Wartburg heights a new torrent of works overflowed: *Commentary on the Magnificat*, *Translation of the New Testament*, *Sermons on the Epistles and Gospels for Sundays and Feast-days*, *On Monastic Vows*, *On the Mass*, *Against Latomus*, the Louvain theologian, *Against the Theologians of Paris*, to whom the events had shown that Luther must be, after all, worthy of condemnation, and who had condemned him, but by-passing silently the question of papal primacy, *Against the Archbishop of Mainz*, who claimed to be starting up again at Halle a treasury of relics producing 40 million years of indulgences, *Against Henry VIII*, King of England, who replied to the *Babylonian Captivity* by defending the doctrine of the seven sacraments, and on whom Leo X would confer the hereditary title of 'Defender of the Faith'.

This is not to say that Luther was really happy at Wartburg. He had long empty periods. The sedentary life sapped him physically and demoralised him: constipation, sexual desires, depressive states, doubts about the past, the present and the future. He could pass days without believing, which was surely a bad sign. He loaded all his anxieties on to the devil's back, and he did so in deadly earnest, a fact which has occupied the attention of his biographers and detractors.

He was increasingly concerned about Wittenberg. Melanch-thon, the dear Elisha, gathered what he could from the Father's mantle. But he gave ground more and more to the general confusion caused by Karlstadt.

Luther's disappearance had turned his colleague's head. For a long time Karlstadt had tolerated the indignities served up at

Leipzig with Duke George's venison. Left to himself, he thought complacently that it was Doctor Karlstadt who had long ago conferred the doctorate on Staupitz's young colt. Once Luther was out of things, it must be clear to everyone that there was now only one genius in Wittenberg. He had stood too long in the shadow of the great man to be accused of lack of modesty.

Having few ideas, he borrowed from Luther the tried and tested method—the spectacular gesture. But what was original and creative with Luther became but a recipe and trick for his pale imitator. The Mass was suppressed, a Saint Bartholomew was made of statues in the churches, the clergy abandoned the rules and took wives.

One day in December, Luther could take it no longer. He escaped from the Wartburg and went to see what was happening at Wittenberg. Only his friends were warned. Cranach made use of it to paint the portrait of 'Junker George'.

On his return, some days later, he dashed off a *Warning to all Christians to guard against Riot and Sedition*. A waste of breath. Disturbing 'prophets' had arrived at Wittenberg from Zwickau, and they stirred up the people against the existing ecclesiastical order. Karlstadt had solemnly celebrated his marriage, after having sent wedding invitations 'to the whole world', and on Christmas Day he had introduced a mass without vestments, without canon or consecration. Families called their sons back from the University and Melanchthon was thinking of packing his bags.

Once again the storm made Luther change course. He had never known how the Wartburg interlude would finish. Charles V was fighting with Francis I and with the Holy See—Francis, officially allied, was intriguing against him behind his back. The Emperor had left Germany and no one seemed to be in a hurry to carry out the chief stipulation of the Edict of Worms. Leo X had not survived the joy which the taking of Parma had brought him, unless poison had got the better of this forty-six-year-old man. In any event, he died on 1 December 1521, leaving to others the necessity of dealing with a huge debt and helping his ruined creditors. The new Pope, Adrian of Utrecht, had not yet left Spain to take up his position at the helm of the Church.

The danger was no greater at Wittenberg than in the eagle's nest of Captain Von Berlepsch. Luther alone was capable of grasping the situation. His place was no longer at the Wartburg. He had perhaps been cowardly at Worms for not saying bluntly what he had to say, in God's name. The time had come to hand over to Providence.

What would the Elector of Saxony say? He was for the moment at the Diet of Nuremberg. Characteristically he had not the least idea what to do after the kidnapping at Möhra. If Luther restored order at Wittenberg, he could only approve. As for the embarrassing questions which the Diet would put to him, he had long since found the means of evading them.

23
The Stranger at the 'Black Bear'

The heavy animal-figure which served as a signboard for the inn swung to and fro in the rain-laden March wind. Drenched and filthy—the streets of Jena were putrid with the excrement of beasts and men—the two travellers pushed open the door,

In the large room of the Black Bear a man was seated at the only table. Tight-fitting trousers, a plain fur doublet, a red leather cape, one corner dragging on the ground: a knight. His hand was resting on the pommel of his sword, and he was reading a book which lay open before him.

Somewhat intimidated, the young men, who were students, settled themselves as best they could on a small bench near the entrance.

'Won't you have a drink?'

Not daring to refuse, they drew near. The ice was soon broken. One of the newcomers made bold to ask for another round. A question from their companion brought them up short.

'You come from Switzerland?'

'Er . . . yes.'

'I thought I recognised your accent. From what part?'

'St Gall.'

'And where are you headed for?'

'Wittenberg, to study.'

'You will find some fellow-countrymen there. Dr Schurf and his brother.'

'Can you tell us if Dr Luther is at Wittenberg? Does anyone know where he is?'

'I know for certain that he is not in Wittenberg. But it shouldn't be long before you see him. You will have an excellent Professor of Greek, master Philip Melanchthon.'

The conversation turned to Erasmus. The stranger was of the opinion that it was always difficult to know what Erasmus was thinking since he lay low and revealed nothing of his thoughts. However, he had a perfect knowledge of Hebrew.

The two students listened open-mouthed to this knight who knew Melanchthon and Erasmus so well and who spiced his remarks with Latin. His black, flashing eyes fascinated them; anyone transfixed with his glance had to turn his eyes away, despite himself.

'Friends, what is being said of Luther in Switzerland?'

'Oh, it's like anywhere else. Some are for, others against. As far as some people are concerned, there is no one better than him. They thank God for having been shown the truth through him. They are glad that they finally know the errors of the past, thanks to him. Others, particularly the clergy, see nothing in him but a dreadful heretic.'

'I see . . . always the priests.'

Growing more confident, one of the young men picked up the book. It was in Hebrew. Abashed, he put it back and the knight pulled it towards him. Surely knights don't read the psalter in Hebrew?

'I would cut off my finger,' said the student, 'to know that language.'

'It can be mastered with a little application. I would like to know it better myself, and I study it every day.'

Night fell. In the half-dark, a silhouette approached. It was the innkeeper, who understood that the two Swiss would like to see Luther.

'Ah, if only you could have arrived two days sooner. He was here, sitting at this very table where you are, in that very place.'

Never had they cursed so much these washed-out, impassable, wearying roads, whose very mud clung to the soles of the feet.

Their disappointment was painful to see.

'At least we have the consolation of sitting at the same table as he, in the same place that he passed through.'

The innkeeper burst out laughing and went out. A moment later, he made a signal from a distance to one of the two students to come and join him,

'I see,' he whispered, 'that you are indeed on Luther's side. That's him, there.'

'A fine joke.'

'It's as I say! But whatever you do, behave as if you know nothing.'

Not at all convinced, being unfamiliar with the Thuringian accent, the young man returned to his compatriot, and at the first possible occasion whispered to him:

'The innkeeper says that it is Luther.'

'You are crazy. He must have said "Hutten"—you didn't understand.'

Hutten? True enough. The dress and the attitude recalled Hutten rather than Luther. Luther was a monk, not a knight. . . . The stranger had lost none of his subtlety. He did his best not to deceive the two men conversing with 'Ulrich von Hutten.'

Meanwhile, two merchants appeared and announced that they would stay the night at the inn. Having taken off their travelling clothes and their spurs, they also drew near. One of them put down beside him an unbound book.

'What is it?' asked the knight.

'Martin Luther's commentary on the Epistles and Gospels. It has just appeared. Don't you know it?'

'I'll get a copy soon.'

'Come,' said the innkeeper, 'the meal is ready.'

The students didn't want to pay a high price, and asked the innkeeper to serve them separately.

'As you wish. Sit with these gentlemen, and I will attend to you separately.'

'Don't do that,' interrupts the knight, 'I'll pay for them.'

During the meal, he was the centre of conversation. His

cheerful and instructive remarks so amazed his companions that they forgot what they were eating. On one occasion, he said, sighing, 'The princes and the nobles are assembled at the Diet of Nuremberg to deal with the Word of God, the Luther case and the miseries of the German nation. But they think of nothing but having a good time. Pretty tournaments, sled-races, debauchery, showing off, women. The fear of God and prayer are the only remedies. But this is what our Christian princes are like!'

He expressed the hope that the true Gospel would bear more fruit with the children and future generations. It was possible now to inculcate the pure truth and the Word of God from the cradle, that is to say, to teach Christians who had never been drugged with the papal poison. Their parents, alas, were practically beyond reform.

The merchants were anxious to put in their word. The older one declared, 'I am not a man of learning and don't understand much of the question either. But it seems to me, whether Luther is an angel of heaven or a demon from hell, that I would like to confess to him, and would pay ten ducats for it. I believe he would be glad to help and could give the comfort which my conscience needs.'

The innkeeper approached the students and murmured: 'Don't trouble yourselves about the bill. Martin has paid it all.'

As the merchants were getting up to go and groom their horses in the stable, the two Swiss thanked the man whom they still took for Ulrich von Hutten. Hearing his name, the knight smiled.

'I've stepped up in the world tonight. These young men take me for Hutten.'

'But,' says the innkeeper, 'it is well known here that you are Martin Luther.'

'There's another good one. They say I am Hutten. You call me Luther. Soon I will be the legendary Markolf!'

And to toast this latest promotion, he filled a large glass with beer. 'Drink up,' he said cheerfully. 'But you two, better take wine, for I know that in Switzerland you are not in the habit of drinking beer and don't care for it.'

Then he rose, gathered up his jacket which he had taken off to make himself comfortable, and took his companions' hands.

'When you are in Wittenberg, greet Dr Schurf for me.'

'Willingly, but he will surely ask from whom. . . .'

'Tell him only this: the one who must come, greets you. He will understand. And now, good evening. I must go to bed.'

The next morning, Luther was up early. He wanted to reach Leipzig as soon as possible, before being recognised. A solitary journey on horseback didn't frighten him. But there was a price on his head, and there was no need to tempt the devil. If he had to die, it might as well be in Wittenberg.

He had no intention of subduing the rioters by force. He had written to Melanchthon: 'Above all, no bloodshed.' This battle was a battle of the Word of God and he wanted to use that weapon alone. He would start again his untiring preaching, and speak every day if necessary.

That was what he was going to say to the Elector. He would hand over to him this ridiculous sword which had nothing to do with him. The Word of God was itself a sword, and was in no need of being defended by a weapon forged by human hands. He who held this doctine from heaven and not from men did not need his line of conduct to be dictated by the powerful ones of this world. He was under a higher protection than that of the Electoral Prince of the Holy Roman Empire. It was he, Luther, who would henceforth take Frederick under his protection.

Strange, and at times dreadful, dreams troubled his nights. His old adversary, the devil, tormented him without respite. He saw himself surrounded by children born of his own flesh. He saw the Pope running out into the streets of Rome, followed by the Emperor's soldiers. Mingling fraternally in pillage and rape and sacrilege, the Spanish infantry and the Lutheran foot-soldiers fulfilled the outlaw's prophecy. Ah, these bestial shrieks of the peasants abandoned to flaying under the indifferent eye of the Catholic bishops and Lutheran princes, reconciled in the defence of their privileges. . . .

But this morning, as on the first day, Luther knew no way of resisting the pressure of the Word of God. He had done nothing. His attitude had never been anything but to yield before the revelation which imposed itself on him. The final consecration to this attitude had been given to him by the Emperor; stripped of his civil status, legally he no longer existed. He was dead. The Word alone had survived. More than ever it was this which he carried with him like a *viaticum*, a holy sacrament. He was going to preach it at Wittenberg, sure in advance of its efficacy.

Why had they tried so forcefully to make him yield? It could only be a matter of divine judgement. Human power came easily to contestors and agitators who followed their own ends. But before the Word of God, this human power was shattered like a vessel thrown on a reef, and broken into a thousand pieces. Luther had no need to fall back on Sickingen's horsemen. The Word, the Word alone had been a great army, a gigantic blaze, an explosive fire of universal dimensions.

By risky meetings in inns, he found out that all, or nearly all, were following him. Others were uncertain, not knowing how to interpret the phenomenon. Neither did he. He went his way, bearing the seeds of death for an out-of-date world, not knowing how to escape from the invincible power surrounding it on every hand. Cochlaeus had reproached him for claiming to be inspired. But could Cochlaeus, the canon of his state, understand what it was to be unable to recant with death in the soul, to renounce the peace and tranquility which are the sweetest blessings which man has?

It was still in spite of himself that he was here, thrown once again alone—very much alone—on the road, God knew for what Apocalypse. The conviction of having identified the Antichrist filled him with terror. For the appearance of the Antichrist announced the end of the world. God would judge the nations. Between now and the last day the Beast, Rome, which was already writhing like a condemned man under the biting attack of the Word, would be run to ground. The new Pope could do nothing about it. Like Leo, the gentle lamb, he would be carried off like a straw into the deadly sewer which was the Curia. The end of the world was on the way and he must go before it.

Having had a bite to eat, he went off to the stable to saddle his horses. A noise of steps, voices. In the doorway appeared the merchants of the previous day. There was an odd air about them.

'Forgive us for the liberty with which we spoke last night about Martin Luther . . .'

The innkeeper had not been able to hold his tongue. He wouldn't run away from the lawsuit which awaited him for having harboured a man under the Ban of the Empire.

'If you happen to confess one day to Luther in person, you will know if it was indeed he with whom you were at table last night.'

Then, making signs for them to move, he led the beast into the yard. With one bound he was in the saddle and spurred on his mount. Soon only the fiery farewell of his cape could be seen, dancing in the morning air like a flame coming to rest.

The two witnesses of his clandestine departure had the same thought: their duty would be to sound the alert, to smother at all costs this torch which was stampeding towards a Germany ready to burst into flames. But they still felt in the depths of their beings the searing wound of his word. This miracle, ever renewed, was perhaps the sole remedy for the mindless pleasures of the princes . . .

They shivered. In their turn, they must choose.

An image rose up irresistibly in their mind, springing straight from that Bible which Luther himself had taught them to read:

'Then I saw heaven opened, and behold, a white horse! He who sat upon it is called Faithful and True, and in righteous-hess he judges and makes war. His eyes are like a flame of fire, and on his head are many diadems; and he has a name inscribed which no one knows but himself. He is clad in a robe dipped in blood, and the name by which he is called is the Word of God. And the armies of heaven, arrayed in fine linen, white and pure, followed him on white horses. From his mouth issues a sharp sword with which to smite the nations, and he will rule them with a rod of iron; he will tread the winepress of the fury of the wrath of God the Almighty. On his robe and on his thigh he has a name inscribed. King of Kings and Lord of Lords . . .

'And I saw the beast and the kings of the earth with their armies gathered to make war against him who sits upon the horse and against his army. And the beast was captured and with it the false prophet who in its presence had worked the signs by which he deceived those who worshipped its image. The rest were slain by the sword of him who sits upon the horse, the sword which issues from his mouth. . . .'

Paris
Feast of the Conversion of St Paul
25 January 1971

X